Become

Become Who God Created You To Be
No Matter What Walk Of Life Or
Season You Are In

Madison Panko

Holman Christian Standard Bible®
Copyright © 1999, 2000, 2002, 2003, 2009 by Holman Bible Publishers.
Used with permission by Holman Bible Publishers, Nashville, Tennessee. All rights reserved.

Scripture quotations marked MSG are taken from THE MESSAGE, copyright © 1993, 2002, 2018 by Eugene H. Peterson. Used by permission of NavPress. All rights reserved. Represented by Tyndale House Publishers, Inc.

THE HOLY BIBLE, NEW INTERNATIONAL VERSION®, NIV® Copyright © 1973, 1978, 1984, 2011 by Biblica, Inc.® Used by permission. All rights reserved worldwide.

NET Bible® copyright ©1996-2017 All rights reserved. Build 30170414 by Biblical Studies Press, L.L.C.

Holy Bible, New Living Translation, copyright © 1996, 2004, 2015 by Tyndale House Foundation. Used by permission of Tyndale House Publishers, Inc., Carol Stream, Illinois 60188. All rights reserved

Book Editing by Jennifer Breeze
Cover Photo by Ashley Masters
Book Design by Presentation Graphics, Inc.

ISBN: 979-8-9877523-4-0 Paperback
ISBN: 979-8-9877523-5-7 Hardcover
ISBN: 979-8-9877523-6-4 Epub

Published by Presentation Graphics Press

Printed in the United States of America

Become

Become Who God Created You To Be
No Matter What Walk Of Life Or
Season You Are In

Madison Panko

Chapter 7: Goodness

🦋 Is there a part of your childhood that was hard? Maybe a divorce, loss of family member or other trauma? Did this event teach you a specific lesson that you think God might want to use as your testimony?

🦋 God wants you to start understanding the hidden goodness in your life, that has always been there even through the harder times of your existence.

I challenge you to start your morning by spending 15 minutes with God every day this week. Soak yourself in the goodness of our Lord by starting your morning in study of His Living Word, devotion and praise. I promise that you will find your day feeling smoother just by enacting this challenge.

🦋 Write out what you did and how you felt while doing this each day this week.

Monday _____

Tuesday _____

Wednesday _____

Thursday _____

Friday _____

Saturday _____

Sunday _____

🦋 Please reach out to three people today, either through a quick text or call, and tell them something that you admire about them. Compliment them and help to spread some goodness into their day.

☐ _____

☐ _____

☐ _____

Discussion Questions

Chapter 1: The Time is Now

- Off the top of your head, what do you envision your Butterfly moment will be?

- What do you feel like you need to do or accomplish before you get your glorious wings?

- Say this out loud for me. "I am a woman of God." C'mon now, I know it sounds silly, but just speak this outloud again. "I AM a woman of God." Last time! Exclaim it with some Gusto! "I AM A WOMAN OF GOD!" Now just in case that didn't sink in enough, I want you to write it out below.

Chapter 2: Love

- In what area of your life do you struggle with giving/relinquishing control over to God?

- How do you feel you can contribute to the Kingdom of Heaven?

- Have you accepted into your heart that you are chosen and loved by God? If not, what do you think is holding you back?

- Journal Prompt: I challenge you to write out areas of your life where you are refusing love, or need to accept God's love. In what ways can you show love to God and others this week?

I invite you to say this prayer with me:
Dear God, I ask that you please enable me to recognize the love that you have for me. That I am able to soak in all your tender compassion towards me. That my heart is able to be softened and I am enabled to love both myself and others in a more pure manner. That the love I have to give is deep and everlasting, just like the love you have for me. Please be with me today and allow me to feel you. I love you Lord. Amen.

Chapter 3: Joy

- I want you to think of a situation that you are currently going through that is hard/difficult. How can you work to find the joy in this area of your life?

- I challenge you to write out three things right now that you are grateful for

- I encourage you to try and say your three gratefuls both before bed and in the morning every day this week. This will help to reposition your heart, and start allowing you to be purposeful with cultivating joy in your life. I challenge you to find the joy in your life by beginning and ending each day with gratitude. Grab a hold of joy tightly and never let it go!

- Have you ever stopped to contemplate the difference between happiness and joy? Compare the two below.

- I challenge you today to make a list of at least 10 occurrences in your life that bring you joy. Not happiness, but tangible moments in your life that God allowed you to experience utter joy. I have done this challenge myself, and what I have found is that the moments of my life that were the most joyful were instances that I could very clearly discern the hand of God working.

Free Resources for You

For assisting you in acknowledging and accepting your
God-given purpose

Companion Study Guide

Deepen your understanding of God's will for your life with these
thought-provoking discussion questions.

These printable worksheets will aid you in either a Bible study
setting or during your own personal time as you allow God to blossom
and grow you.

Download your Study Guide here:

Dedication

This book is dedicated to my wonderful husband, Jake.

For without his supportive encouragement and wholehearted enthusiasm, I would still be staring at a blank document. Thank you for believing in me, even when I didn't believe in myself.

Your love has helped to soften my rough edges and allowed me to blossom. Without you I wouldn't have the courage to be vulnerable.

Thank you for being my adventure partner for life. You're the best, Love Dove. God has truly blessed me with the most epic best friend.

I'll love you forever, and slow dance to Frank Sinatra with you until eternity.

My Prayer For You

Dear God,

Please uplift the woman who is reading this book right now. Please knock on the door of her heart, soothe her weary soul, and wash a current of calm over her mind. Prince of Peace, please wrap your child into your sweet delightful angel wings. Please shelter and protect your flock. Please allow these words to fall on good soil, and for the messages that you have allowed to speak through me into this book to be truly heard and well-received. Allow seeds to be planted and your Good News to be reaped.

Lord, you are so mighty and worthy of all our praise. Let us recognize the best ways we can serve your kingdom. Please help your followers to understand the mission that you uniquely put them on this Earth for. Please help my sweet sister who is reading this to figure out what she needs to do, work on, or embrace in order to become who you crafted her to be. Please help her to discover her wings and allow her to fly higher than she ever even dreamed to be possible.

Simply, enable and strengthen her to Become. Her time is now.

In Jesus' Name, Amen.

Table of Contents

Dedication i

My Prayer for You.. ii

CHAPTER 1: The Time is Now 13

CHAPTER 2: Love 23

CHAPTER 3: Joy 39

CHAPTER 4: Peace 53

CHAPTER 5: Patience 61

CHAPTER 6: Kindness 79

CHAPTER 7: Goodness.. 91

CHAPTER 8: Faith 103

CHAPTER 9: Gentleness... 111

CHAPTER 10: Self-Control 123

CHAPTER 11: Comprehending Catastrophe....................................... 149

CHAPTER 12: Become the Butterfly 173

A Prayer for New Life 182

About the Author.. 184

Different is admirable. Unique is ravishing. Embrace the unthinkable, because you were meant not to blend in, but to be distinct and exceptional.

The Time Is Now

These words have been inscribed on my heart for a very long time. Yet being the type of woman I am, constantly looking for my sunglasses when they are already on top of my frazzled head; I wasn't able to recognize the calling of God's message for my life until it was so obvious that it was laughable.

I have a story to share. It is a story of heartbreak, sin, and devastation. But I am not unique in this unfolding drama, as I feel we all have a similar skeleton in our own closet. One that we try to forget about; attempting to mask the rotting corpse inside by throwing garments on top of it.

I used to act like I was perfect. Little miss everything, trying to convince myself that if I looked perfect on the outside, then just maybe I could con myself into being it on the inside. My answer would always be the same to the proverbial question that many of us get asked multiple times a day, "How are you doing?"

Insert fake smile and robotic automatic response of "Oh, I'm good!" or "Doing great! How about you?"

I used to believe that by not sharing my struggles, maybe I could begin to feel like they weren't real. Like the weight of them would no longer be a burden upon my shoulders.

I have so often tried to fit into a cookie-cutter mold. To cram myself in there, ashamed and discouraged when my edges wouldn't bend a certain way.

Why couldn't I be like the status quo? Why couldn't I just be normal?

But God showed me that by living in constant comparison, I was rejecting the design He had created for me. An intricate and unique mold that only I could fill.

Ladies, normal is overrated! After you have been through a certain number of events, normal just doesn't fit into your vocabulary. Like a foreign language that you neither understand nor yearn to comprehend.

I used to believe the lie from the enemy that I should be like everyone else. That because I was different, thought different, and felt different, I was somehow wrong. Faulty.

A mistake.

This very sin kept me trapped and broken for longer than I would like to admit. I fell for the sham of should.

I should work this job. I should be more like her. I should enjoy doing the same things that everyone else seems to enjoy. I should make this much money. I should dress like this. I should weigh this much. I should have this type of personality.

NO!

The only thing I SHOULD be is who God created me to be.

The unique, eccentric, and sometimes unpredictable daughter of Christ. Prized child, carefully and purposefully crafted to be different.

> *"Do not be conformed to this age, but be transformed by the renewing of your mind, so that you may discern what is good, pleasing, and perfect will of God." (Romans 12:2 HCSB)*

Don't be alarmed, my story is not all doom and gloom. So put away those tissues! This is actually a tale of redemption. One filled with hope and love, an abundance of forgiveness and grace. Like the verse from one of my favorite worship songs *Amazing Grace*, "I once was lost, but now I'm found."

Now, I know who I am. The prized name that my Heavenly Father calls me. I know that I need to ignore the shouts of should.

That my motto is not to try, but to become.

This is the journey set out for each one of us. We all have our own adventure to embark upon, filled with discovery.

Spoiler Alert: The hidden treasure is your salvation, already earned and paid for by Jesus Christ.

Find this treasure, destined for you. It has your very name inscribed upon it. Step into the shoes the Lord has designed and set in front of you. No one else can wear them, they are meant for you alone to walk into.

Personally, my shoes would look like a pair of black combat boots, and yours most likely look very different. And that's part of the beauty of it.

Different is admirable. Unique is ravishing. Embrace the unthinkable, because you were meant not to blend in, but to be distinct and exceptional.

The Butterfly Effect A Radical Transformation

I can't quite pinpoint exactly when this obsession began, but I have had a love affair with butterflies for as long as I can remember. You see, the butterfly is a magnificent creature, arguably one of the most vibrant and stunning creations within God's Kingdom.

I am in awe just thinking about all of the revolutionary transformations that take place during this insect's brief lifecycle here on Earth. Butterflies, as I'm sure you know, develop through a process called metamorphosis. However, no matter how mesmerizing their jeweled wings become, it is important to note that these dramatic beings were not initially created with this exquisite design.

As children, many of us learn about this amazing process in easy to understand lingo. As bright eyed, ready-to-take-on-the-world adolescents, we marvel at the majestic magic that the butterfly seems to possess. If you were lucky enough to have a 3rd grade teacher like mine, you actually had a pet butterfly in your classroom for a time. You were able to watch the growing process from the microscopic egg, to a weak caterpillar, to a strange white coffin looking thing (the chrysalis), and then astonishingly to a beautiful butterfly stretching its gorgeous wings and begging to be set free.

I remember the exact moment that my class and I excitedly pranced outside, skipping with joy ready to release our exotic butterfly into the world. It was such a special moment when the lid to the cage was lifted and said butterfly took its first flight. Flitting around gracefully towards the aqua blue sky, its radiant colors complementing the bright flower-filled ambiance of the late spring season that was among us.

In that moment, I remember wishing I could be the very independent butterfly I was gazing at. Free to fly wherever the wind carried me, radiating joy, a true sight to see for all who beheld me.

What an exhilarating thought. One day I hoped to be able to turn from the small leaf-munching caterpillar stuck on the ground, to a hope-filled butterfly, able to travel to heights greater than I even imagined to be possible.

To transform from a state of surviving to a place of thriving.

In Austin, Texas where I grew up, we are blessed by an influx of monarch butterflies flitting about everywhere. For a certain season, especially during the very late summer months, they appear all over. As a young girl, I remember finding their little dead bodies all over the yellowing grass. Unfortunately, butterflies don't live very long, as these beautiful creatures only have a few brief weeks before their time on Earth has expired.

I would gently collect all of their bodies and give them a proper funeral of sorts. However, as the ever-curious child that I was, I remember imagining what their wings felt like, dying to stroke the auburn wings in front of me. Ever so carefully, I brushed my small plump fingers across the delicate surface area of one of the deceased monarch's wings and gasped. Their intricate wings felt like silk to my fingertips, smooth and buttery like liquid.

These tiny creatures are so detailed in design, with everything about them, even their lifecycle being extremely interesting and complex.

Do you know the entire in-depth process that a caterpillar goes through in order to become a butterfly? If not, I'll give you a brief synopsis. The larva (caterpillar) is hatched from an egg. It then spends much of its life as a creepy crawly consuming leaves and food, to prepare for its impending big transformation. During this time of eating and growth the caterpillar grows bigger and stronger through a series of molts, in which it sheds its previous skin. Alas, the day comes when the chubby caterpillar's insatiable appetite wanes and the creature relocates to hang upside down from a twig or a leaf, spinning a cocoon in which it can transform safely.

Although invisible to the outside eye, a complete metamorphosis is taking place inside that tiny, seemingly unimpressive, and insignificant cocoon. Eventually, the caterpillar is radically transformed and its body emerges as a new creature, spectacular and stunning.

You would never know, by looking at a slimy little caterpillar that a whimsical butterfly was awaiting undiscovered inside.

We are much like the caterpillar-to-butterfly transition. Our lives take place in stages, with each stage having a specific purpose. For the longest time, I yearned, hoped, and reverently prayed that I would alas transition into the splendid butterfly that I knew I was meant to become.

For me, this insect metamorphosis was not only personal, but painstakingly frustrating. Over time, when I would think I was finally at that point where I was in my cocoon, all dark and changing, I would realize with dismay that no, I was still the same measly caterpillar as before, molting another layer of my skin. Shedding a part of my old self and although growing bigger and stronger, I was still more or less untransformed.

I never knew when or if ever, my revolutionary wings would come. If I would ever be able to say with certainty, "This is it. I have finally become the butterfly."

Adventure Awaits

This book is for you. No matter what season, age, or walk of life you're currently in.

My story could be your story - maybe you too have made mistakes that you wish didn't exist. Maybe you also have been through some unimaginable challenges, events that you thought would break you but in reality, were destined to make you stronger.

> *"There's more to come: We continue to shout our praise even when we're hemmed in with troubles, because we know how troubles can develop passionate patience in us, and how that patience, in turn, forges the tempered steel of virtue, keeping us alert for whatever God will do next."*
> *(Romans 5:3 MSG)*

I have found that although women are all unique, beautiful, and complex, the undertone of our pain is very similar. Many of us struggle with loss, acceptance, grief, bitterness, forgiveness, and hurts that have wounded us to our core. Anxiety and depression are running rampant in our society; with us women being especially plagued with feelings of inadequacy. So many of us are lost in a sea of lies, that we are worthless, undeserving, and not good enough. That we just can't measure up.

This lie could not be further from the truth! We are loved, treasured, and capable.

We are called to be Warriors for God. We are not little girls, we are strong, resilient, and unbreakable women. I am a Woman of God. A Warrior Princess for the Highest King. And you are called to be too.

Through my heartbreak, I have discovered my true name. Through my sin, I was lost to the world, but Jesus found me and offered me a hand. He pulled me out of the dark pit I resided in and now I sit among royalty.

God wants, more than anything in the world, for YOU to become who He created you to be. For you to recognize the beauty inside of yourself, the untapped potential, and unfailing strength that He built you with. The spiritual gifts you have been graciously given and the servant heart you're meant to use to help countless others discover the truth.

Whether you are single, married, or widowed, it's not too late. Whether you are a college student still figuring out the world or an empty-nester searching for a new purpose, the time is now.

You are holding this book for a reason. Jesus is using this book as an instrument to reach you.

Yes, YOU.

You are cherished, beloved one. You have a purpose that no one else can fulfill, a destiny that was only gifted to you alone. It's never too late to walk unafraid into the light. Scratch that, sprint to it my talented friend, and never look back.

Your legacy is calling.

We are each called to be a vessel. To spread light and love. The good news is too good not to share.

I'll be the first to tell you, sweet sister, that the best decision I ever made was to allow God to have my heart. I placed that weary, torn, and beaten thing into His hands and He made me whole. I am a new creature, crafted beautifully from light. My past is dead, forever put away, and it will not hold me down any longer. More than anything, I pray the same for you.

> *"But the fruit of the Spirit is love, joy, peace, patience, kindness, goodness, faithfulness, gentleness and self-control. Against such things there is no law." (Galatians 5:22-23 NIV)*

This is one of my all-time favorite verses. After rededicating my life to Christ, I've held this verse very dear to me. I have been working hard to embody each aspect of the Fruit of the Spirit, for it is my goal that my character always reflects these holy sentiments. You see, these nine qualities make up the Fruit of the Spirit, as they are all parts to one whole. You cannot embody the Fruit of the Spirit without learning to cultivate each of its characteristics.

The Fruit is enacted by the Spirit developing through us. When we wholeheartedly yield ourselves to God's Spirit, His Fruit will be born through our thoughts, actions, and everyday decisions. This process is two-fold, being both organic and cultivated. Evidence of our spiritual maturity is displayed through the Fruit that we bear. By exhibiting the Fruit of the Spirit, we are enabling God to manifest through our transformed hearts and souls. In order for God to deepen our character, we must make the conscious decision to die to self, every single day. Yes, there are growing pains that come along with this selfless act. But when the Fruit of the Spirit is evidently displayed in our lives, this is a direct sign that we are being led by the Spirit of the Lord.

> *"I am the vine; you are the branches. If you remain in me and I in you, you will bear much fruit; apart from me you can do nothing." (John 15:5 NIV)*

This statement from Jesus took me a while to comprehend, as our God is not a God of scraps. He is an all-or-nothing God. He does not want us to walk the line, dancing between what is Holy and what is of the world.

> *"Do not love this world nor the things it offers you, for when you love the world you do not have the love of the Father in you." (1 John 2:15 NLT)*

We are not called to be lukewarm Christians. We are designed to be bold in our faith, and this is my prayer every day for both myself and you all.

But I am not perfect. I still make mistakes. I still sin sometimes, and I definitely have too much sass at others. I am human, born from sin. This way of life is an ongoing growth process. I'm not going to be that person who lies and says that one day you will reach this heavenly threshold where you no longer have to work on growing closer to God. It's a daily conscious decision to dedicate your life to the Lord.

This is a journey. A quest for greatness. The grandest adventure you could ever decide to embark upon.

Want to know the best part?

You will never have to do it alone! Jesus will walk hand-in-hand with you the entire way. God will protect you, like the greatest shepherd of all, watching over His flock. And the Holy Spirit will reside inside of you, guiding, teaching, and reminding you which turns to take along this glorious route.

And I am here for you. I am praying for you. I have a deep desire, a serious yearning to grow my God-community. To flourish and strengthen within a tribe of women who know their Heavenly Father and embrace the love He so generously offers.

I love you, encourage you, and challenge you to not just read these chapters but embrace them. To accept what God is trying to communicate to you through them. Let Jesus tattoo His words onto the tapestry of your heart. Allow these messages to water your soul. Turn to the Holy Spirit for insight on how you too can begin to embody the Fruit of the Spirit and how this book can assist you on your journey of becoming.

Are you ready to become the woman God created you to be?

That's the spirit!

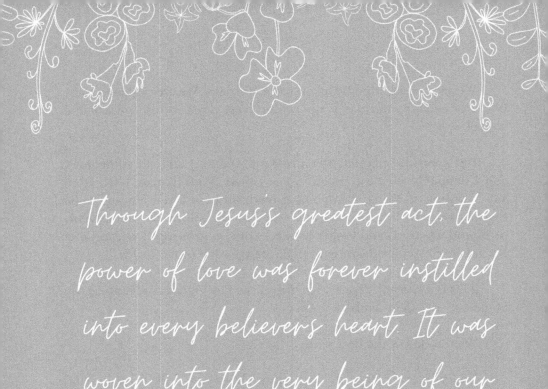

Through Jesus's greatest act, the power of love was forever instilled into every believer's heart. It was woven into the very being of our souls. We were created out of love and we were saved through love. Thus, love is the greatest thing we could ever share while we are here on Earth.

G od created love. He is the author and sculptor of the very essence that all of love embodies. Thus, real love is only capable of being tapped into when we are pulling from the source of our Heavenly Father.

The love of God can be displayed through the love that resides in you and is exhibited and shared with the rest of the world. The more love you have to give is in direct correlation with how close you are to your all-loving and compassionate Father.

We should stop throwing around blanket terms like, "God bless you." And instead, allow God to work through us to actually bless those people. To ask God to use us as an instrument, blessing all of those that we encounter in whichever way the Holy Spirit is guiding us.

My first love was a very volatile relationship. As lovesick teenagers, we believed we were destined to be together. Our craziness and addictive inclinations meshed to create a potent combination of unhealthy obsession with one another.

This relationship very quickly turned toxic and abusive. The emotional and physical abuse took nearly a decade to overcome, and when the relationship first ended I was filled with an immense amount of both grief and hatred.

I hated myself for allowing this neglect and disuse of my heart to continue for as long as it did. And I hated him for "ruining" me. For taking advantage of my young and naive heart, and creating a jaded broken person out of me.

It took a lot of counseling and coming to God on my knees for me to come to a place of forgiveness. And although that man in my past was unfair to me, I was also a very unhealthy person in his life too. I had to learn to recognize my own mistakes and forgive myself. And I also had to work very hard to overcome my anger and forgive my ex.

Now I have love for him. Do I love him? No, not in the romantic sense. But I have love for the mistreated boy who was so hurt by his childhood that he in turn hurt others. My love towards him comes from God, as God wants me to see that he was so broken by his own past that he took out that anger on me.

I have forgiven him. I have let all of that hate in my heart go. God has helped me to move on and put this part of my past behind me. I still sometimes pray for him. I pray that his childhood will no longer seep into his present. I pray that he will not treat another woman the way he treated me. I pray that when he is a father that he will not treat his children the way that his father treated him.

I pray that He is able to find the redeeming love of His Heavenly Father and live a blessed life.

Talking of God's love is meaningless unless we also display it toward others. Action is the true testament to how faithfully you are walking with Christ. We can display God's love by laying down our lives for His cause. By being bold in things that make us uncomfortable, fearless in standing up for the truth, and never ceasing to share the love that God has for all His children.

Christ's sacrifice is proof of God's dedicated love for you. God gave His one and only Son, allowing Him to endure the worst of treatment and torture so that you could be forgiven of your sins.

Isn't that kind of crazy to actually sit down and contemplate?

Imagine if you had a precious child, that you chose to send away to live somewhere far from you. And you knew, by sending your only baby to that place, that your little one would end up suffering more than anyone else in mankind. But you also knew, that if you did not make the selfless sacrifice of your beloved child, that many more people for the rest of time would end up suffering also. Would you allow your adorable little angel to go off, away from you, and end up dying for other people's wrongdoings? Would you be able to stand by as your son grew up and was mocked, plotted against, and bitterly abused? Would you be able to watch as your son, grown into a stunning young man, was beaten to a pulp, stripped naked, and nailed to a cross in front of despicable people who tormented your darling up until he took his last pained breath?

Would you have been able to make that sacrifice? Would you have been able to give up the thing you loved most in the world, your only offspring, for people who were undeserving?

I don't personally have any babies yet. But I have wanted them since I was a little girl. I am fiercely protective of all children, even those who aren't my own kin. Every time I am in a public place, whenever I hear a child crying my ears instantly perk up and I look to see if I can be of any help to the little one in distress. Many times, I have approached overwhelmed mothers on planes and held their babies so they could get some rest. Soothing a child is one of the things in life that I take the most pleasure in.

If I am this protective over children who aren't even mine, I can't even begin to imagine what I will be like with my own little slices of Heaven. The thought of relinquishing my child to a fate like Jesus, is utterly unfathomable to me.

When I look at Jesus's journey on Earth from the perspective of God, I am humbled to my knees at the realization of the sacrifice that He allowed to happen. That selfless act of a Father and of an obedient willing Son, makes my eyes water at the true love that they both displayed.

I am not worthy of this. But somehow, my Heavenly Father deemed me so. Through Jesus's greatest act, the power of love was forever instilled into every believer's heart. It was woven into the very being of our souls.

We were created out of love and we were saved through love. Thus, love is the greatest thing we could ever share while we are here on Earth.

> *"And hope does not disappoint, because the love of God has been poured out in our hearts through the Holy Spirit who was given to us." (Romans 5:5 NET)*

Understanding And Accepting

I used to have a very hard time loving myself. In my past, I made so many mistakes, acted upon so many uncountable sins, that I thought I didn't deserve love. Definitely not from others, but especially not from myself.

I have lied, stolen, and cheated. I used to be a master manipulator. I have betrayed people that I cared deeply for. And I have chosen my alcohol addiction over those I have loved. The immense amount of shame that I used to carry around weighed down my soul, suppressed the Holy Spirit, and blocked out all light.

There was a long period where I refused to look at myself in the mirror. I would go into the bathroom, go about my getting ready business, but avert my eyes from the mirror at all costs.

Heck, after a couple of good pokes to the eye with the mascara wand, I even learned how to put on my makeup without looking! I didn't want to face the monster I had created of myself. The temptations I had succumbed to had hardened my heart, to the point where I no longer recognized who I was.

Because of this self-loathing, I began to treat myself even worse than I had before. You see, I have realized that the two most dangerous things in the world are being unable to love yourself and unwilling to see the devoted love that God has for you.

I was denying the first, and unintentionally shunning the second.

I would act in self-sabotaging manners with substances and promiscuity, justifying in my mind that I didn't deserve happiness. A sinner like me was meant to be miserable, that alone would be a fitting punishment. I wish I could tell you that this period lasted for a few months, but in all honesty, I lived in a self-hate state for a multitude of desolate years.

Only by the grace of God, some serious Christian counseling, and drawing closer to the Lord through devotion and prayer, was I able to come to a place of forgiveness and redemption. It was not an overnight acceptance, and it has taken me a very long time to learn to look at myself not as the sinner I was, but as the saved child I am.

I can finally look in the mirror without despising my reflection because now the person looking back at me is a woman clothed in strength, dignity, and love.

We all have regrets. Things we have said or done that we wish we hadn't. I used to wish I could push the rewind button on my life, erasing all of the things I wanted to take back. But then God mercifully revealed to me that I would not be here, right here right now, writing this very book, if that wish was to be granted. My past is my testimony, the gate that is going to help me to encourage and relate to others like me who have also struggled.

I used to think that I was so much worse than everyone else. That my sins were immensely dirtier and therefore I was lesser because of them. But God spoke to me, He soothingly comforted my lost mind, reminding me that I was His sweet child. And that we have all fallen short of the glory of God. That sin is sin in the Lord's eyes, and mine was no messier than anyone else's.

"for all have sinned and fall short of the glory of God," (Romans 3:23 NIV)

Become

Gift From God

Sometimes when I think of love, I think of my fur baby Stella. She, on a daily basis, reminds me what genuine love should look like.

I was 18 years old, fresh out of high school, and making more bad decisions than I can list on both hands. I was preparing to go off to college in San Antonio, and I was very nervous as I knew no one there and the closest friend that I had was an on-again-off-again toxic boyfriend that I ended up having to get a protective order against.

I was spending one of my last summer days left, with my younger sister Maryn. And although the luminous sun was glistening down on us, all I had felt that day was impending doom and gloom. One of the things that I liked to do at that time (okay you got me, and still now) when I was feeling sad was to visit the animal shelter and cuddle with some kittens.

You see, I have been a cat lover ever since Santa gifted me with my childhood best friend at the age of 4. Years later, my Mom revealed to me the actual story behind Santa's gift, and I was horrified. My precious little kitty was adopted off the side of the road from the back of a van. But the piece of the story that had always stuck out to me was that my Mom had looked at other kittens, but none had given her "that" feeling.

When she picked up what would become my childhood best friend, the tiny fluff melted into a ball of butter in her arms, nuzzling in tight. Even though loud cars were zooming angrily past on the highway, even though it was a stranger and the situation couldn't have been more stressful, my little kitten had trusted the hands she was placed in and accepted her new home with grace, gratitude, and love.

My kitten Vixen (named after one of Santa's reindeer) was my very best friend growing up. She would sleep with me every night, lick my tears away when I was sad, and always provided a therapeutic sounding board, listening to the woes of a child who was growing up torn back and forth between households. She was my good girl, and I had her for a wonderful 13 years before we had to make the hard decision to put her down after cancer had riddled her body.

Since Vixen, there had never been another animal that I had grown exceptionally close to. As an animal lover at heart, sure I would love on just about anything that breathed (except frogs—eww) but the spiritual connection that I felt with Vixen was never rekindled.

Thinking back, I know that God gave me that kitty as a little guardian angel. In a time when I felt so alone in a house full of people, she was there to remind me that I was loved and cared for. That I did matter and wasn't invisible.

I never thought I would find another kitty like Vixen, as she was an exceptionally brilliant feline. She turned out to be a Maine Coon, with a majestic lion's mane, long flowing fur, and striking green eyes that seemed to be able to read my soul. Everyone who met her would comment on how beautiful of a cat she was, and how loyal she was to her mother. In a house of five, Vixen was mine and mine alone. When I would be away at my Dad's, sometimes for weeks at a time. Vixen would mourn me, still sleeping at the foot of my bed every night and occasionally crying loudly inside my empty room.

I remember talking with Maryn that summer day as we were driving to the Georgetown Animal Shelter, reminiscing on my childhood animal. Wishing more than anything I could have her with me as I embarked on the next journey of my life. Ending my chapter of living at home and soon leaving for college filled me with so much uncertainty and anxiety toward the unknowns of my future.

In all honesty, this was probably the 17th animal shelter I had visited throughout that summer. Like I mentioned above, when I felt sad, one of the only healthy outlets I had at the time, was holding kittens and loving on something that wanted my love. Although kittens are great fun, I was not interested in getting another kitty unless I were to get that same feeling that Vixen gave my Mother the first time she was held.

You see, if you've never had a kitten or aren't much of a cat person then I best explain. Kittens are little rascals, think puppy but with like 15x the energy. They are like little Tasmanian devils that want to explore every nook and cranny and then climb up your pant leg. They are just learning how to exercise their voice, so they will talk to you constantly, and they very rarely relax until they have tuckered themselves out and then they fall into a little kitten coma in the most hilarious positions until they're recharged and ready to run rampant again.

I love the bottomless energy of a kitten, which is why they make me feel so much better when I am in a depressive state. However, I would be lying if I didn't admit that I was secretly hoping that one day I would get the same feeling of love, trust, and tenderness that Vixen had first displayed. Every encounter with a new kitten began much the same, I would pick the little thing up, attempt to cradle it like a baby in my arms, and then set the wild child back down again. They would always squirm or squeal in protest, not wanting to rest but to play. Playing was great fun but I was looking for a kindred spirit who could be in a restful state with me when my heart was feeling low.

That day Maryn and I held each and every kitten (or so we thought), each of them screaming to be held and then struggling to be let down so they could run and tackle their playmates once again. After exhausting our kitten options, I was ready to leave. Head down, feet heavily shuffling, and feeling like the weight of the world was on my shoulders, I trudged grumpily towards the glass adoption center exit doors.

"Wait, what about this one!" My darling sister shouted.

The squeak of my boots echoed in the tiled hallway as I spun quickly around looking to where my sister was staring. Hidden in plain sight, as my wonderful sister pointed out (thank you a million times over Maryn) there was still one kitten left undiscovered. This scrawny little thing was fast asleep in the farthest cage, oblivious to the world. I had completely overlooked this content unconscious baby, because it wasn't begging for attention like all the others.

At first I wasn't even going to bother holding it, as it obviously didn't want to be disturbed. But Maryn encouraged me, so I reached into the cage and picked up the petite creature. She was such a tiny little thing, fitting inside one hand, and definitely not the most stunning from her litter.

I robotically enacted the same process as I always did, attempting to cradle the small creature into my arms. However, this time something miraculous happened. The kitten snuggled into the crevice of my arms, drawing nearer to my bodice. She stretched her miniature self out, opened her precious eyes, and just gazed at me like I held the keys to the entire world.

Ya'll… my heart melted.

In that brief millisecond, I just knew. This was the feeling I had been searching for, this kitten was meant for me and me alone. Right here, right now, I had to have her.

Granted, I totally didn't have the money to pay for her adoption fee and my parents had already specifically stated that I was not allowed to come home with a kitten, as I was about to live in a dorm where no pets were allowed. But I was determined, stubbornly in kitten love, and gosh darn it, I was going to find a way.

I called my Dad and as the teenager that I still was, I begged. No shame. He absolutely refused, making the fatal mistake of stating that I would not be allowed to take said kitten to my dorm with me. As an entrepreneur at heart, with a stubborn side, I rose to the challenge.

Determined, I called my counselor, who agreed that it was a great idea to have a companion animal, and sent over a letter stating that it would be in my best interest to bring an emotional support animal to college with me. And then I called my campus, explaining the situation. They stated that although it would be a process, as long as I had the necessary paperwork then it would be permitted.

All that was left was the price, initially $125. I walked up to the counter, still holding said precious kitten, afraid to let her go. I passionately explained that this kitten and I were destined for each other. I made a very valiant speech, and lobbied grandiosely my ability to be a splendid cat-mother while trying to bargain down the price.

The older lady chuckled, making her pastel pink glasses bob on the bridge of her nose. Then she kindly stated that I was in luck. Today only, they were doing a $13 cat adoption special, with all shots and the spay included. Maryn was in utter disbelief that I had somehow pulled this all off. Meanwhile, I was ecstatic and my precious little miracle kitty was still peacefully cozied up in her new Mother's arms.

I ended up naming my fur baby Stella Luna, after one of my favorite childhood books about a lovable baby bat. Although initially scrawny and ragged, my tiny Stella grew into the most majestic creature. Unknown to us all, she too was a Maine Coon. She is almost a carbon copy of Vixen, with a full lion's mane and sparkling inquisitive green eyes. She gives me kisses when I am melancholy and sleeps on the right corner at the foot of my bed, just like Vixen used to.

Stella has been with me through my hardest adult years, faithfully showing me love even when I could not love myself. My "fluffy butt", as I refer to her, is my 18-pound guardian angel, and she is cuddled up to my side right now as I write this. In our 8-years together she has taught me many valuable lessons.

When adopted, she initially did not look like much. She was sometimes skittish, timid, and afraid, so unused to the love I was wishing to bestow upon her. I too was like that with God, unwilling to accept the tenderness that He was trying to show me. But once Stella allowed me to be her parent, she began to blossom and grow. Now she is a powerhouse of beauty and grace. She commands the attention of a room and is not shy in the skin (more like— mass amount of fur) that she was born into. She now understands that she deserves love, that her whole purpose in life is to love and be loved.

This is the command that Jesus has placed on us too. We are to accept the love of our Father, the ultimate act of love through Jesus's sacrifice and we are to bestow that same level of love to everyone we encounter.

Fluffy butt has some sass at times, and the start to our relationship was trial and error, to say the least. It took stubborn Stella a good while to accept and respect that I was the one in charge, but eventually she acknowledged that I was the alpha female in our family.

We too need to accept that God has authority. He is the one in charge. No ifs, ands, or buts about it. When we yell, cuss, and throw spiritual tantrums, our Father still opens His arms and beckons us to Him. But just like Stella will always be my rambunctious fur baby, we will always be God's children.

The hierarchy is not alterable. We have to learn to stop having a power-struggle with our all-powerful God. There's no competition!

Once I let God take His rightful role as my Heavenly Father, I began to flourish. I am naked and unafraid before the all-knowing eyes of the Lord. While I used to be more of a closet Christian, hiding my faith in the shadows, I know now that is not where God is calling me to serve. The Lord gave me a voice, so that I could raise it and speak life-giving words of truth. He invoked me with a passion for writing, so that I could write what the Holy Spirit wills me to. I am simply a vessel with which God can use how He pleases.

We are also kind of like the crazy kittens gallivanting wildly around at the shelter. So often we are too busy running rampant, asking for attention but then refusing to stay still in the silence of the one who wishes to love us most. We are too busy to just stop and accept the love that is being freely offered to us, with no strings attached. If only those hundreds (yes, it really was hundreds) of kittens had allowed me to hold them, and been content to relax in the stillness I was offering, then they would have found their forever home. They would have been given the thing that each of them had been loudly whining for, a true family. But they were unwilling to be patient, to accept the love that was being shown to them because it was not being shown in the way they wanted.

Isn't that so like us?

We want love, but if it doesn't show up wrapped in a package to our liking, then we reject it. So often God would try and bestow His love on me, but I was unwilling to alter my plans and stop what I was doing to accept it.

The kittens who only wanted to play were much like how I used to be. All about fun and receiving gifts of love in ways that were most suiting to me. However, love is actually all about being selfless. I needed to stop thinking of God from the perspective of what could He do for me and change it to what can I do for Him?

How could I contribute to the Kingdom of Heaven?

I had to learn that love is about giving freely, without expectation or reward. It's allowing God to shine through you in order to show others how cherished and valuable they are. Love is an ongoing display that actively compels us to put others' needs before the comfort of our own.

Not A Feeling, But An Action

Love is a word that is so commonly thrown around that it has almost lost its pizzazz. I love my steaming cup of coffee that I am currently sipping on, I love the shoes the worship leader at church was wearing yesterday, I love bargain shopping for old records from the 70s. I love my husband. I love the Lord.

You see how this single word is intertwined in both such a worldly and spiritual way? There are connotations to both.

The sinful nature of us lusts and loves after things, tangible items that we incorrectly associate with a spiritual feeling. The want for more. We so often find ourselves distracted with the shiny temptation of thinking that we need something (a big house, a large diamond ring, a sports car, a luxury vacation, the newest iPhone etc. etc.) in order to be happy or feel like we have made it in life.

This could not be further from the truth!

What we NEED, is to learn how to accept and embrace the love of our Heavenly Father. We need to desire and learn more about how to embody the teachings of love that Jesus demonstrated in the New Testament. We need the Holy Spirit to fill us with so much love, that we are an overflowing fountain, tenderly caring for those around us.

Do you see how many of us have our priorities backwards? This confusion is seeping into the very essence of the most important lesson that Jesus ever taught. How love is the greatest of all things.

> *"Three things will last forever — faith, hope, and love — and the greatest of these is love." (1 Corinthians 13:13 NLT)*

This day and age is filled with the wrong type of love. The kind of love that is a sham. A love-hate where one minute you're on top of the world and the next you're signing divorce papers. One minute where you're adored by many fans and sponsored by big brands, only to make one mistake and instantly become a disliked has-been.

This is not love from God. God's love is perfect, unshakable, and never failing. He will never take back his love for you.

This is a no-return policy.

God's love is righteous because His love is not a simple feeling. Love is persevering, honorable, and hopeful. It is trusting and unfaltering. The amount of love you have and give out is a direct correlation to how close you are to the Father because without love we are nothing. You are not obediently walking the ways of the Spirit without a loving overflowing heart.

Dive Off The Deep End With Me

The Lord clearly instructs us that the greatest of all of things is love.

Learning to love and be loved by our Heavenly Father is the first step from this book that I want to emphasize. It is impossible to become who you were truly created to be, if you shut out your Creator!

Our Creator holds the blueprint to our lives, the roadmap to our happiness, and the instruction manual on how to fulfill our purpose.

It's like when our car breaks and we try to fix it ourselves. But the driving manual is in a totally different language, that even Google translate can't decipher, and we keep botching the repair job in one way or another. Why would we not just take our car to the manufacturer himself? The Creator who birthed this project into the world, who knows every nook and cranny of His creation?

You see where I'm going here?

No self-help book will allow you alone to interpret the mission of your existence. Only through God, your designer, can you find the answers and undeniable peace that your soul has been searching for.

The first step to learning your purpose, is to embrace the unarguable fact that you are chosen and loved. Accepting this truth will utterly alter the course of your life for the better.

Instead of wobbling around, tripping, and stumbling, like you're in a carnival house with shaky floors. You will be able to walk on solid ground, sturdy and strong in the knowledge that you are loved and cherished. No matter what you have done.

The fact of the matter is, none of us deserve it!

I got caught up on this caveat for so long, knowing full well I did not deserve God's love, thus I was unwilling to allow myself to accept it. But that's actually the point, this gift of grace is what God is all about! He will love us no matter what. He will bestow his mercy upon even the most undeserving folk, such as myself.

By learning to accept God's love, I not only became spiritually more lovable, but also, his contagious overflow of tender love began to spill out into every area of my life. I no longer "loved" the things in my life, but I began to love the people around me, people in need, and even people I had never met that were very different from myself.

God's love will fill you to the brim, so full that you will find it impossible to contain this raw revealing emotion, and you too will find it impossible to not also spread light and love all around you!

My heart has been healed and made new again. The love I have to give is more strong, sincere, and tender than it ever was before. And that's because my love is no longer coming from the shallow kiddie pool of the world, but from a bottomless expanse of crystal clear, life-giving, and refreshing living water.

I encourage you to sip from this satisfying water and be made brand new.

When you allow joy from God into your heart, you find the ability to commandeer the emotions that used to control you.

Joy

J oy is a state of being, not a feeling. It is a place in which your soul resides that no human, event, or circumstance can remove you from. When you are truly joyful, you are able to rejoice in all things, even the hardest moments of life. This is because joy is not a mood. Happiness may come and go, flitting around like the wind, but joy is a state of residing in the presence of the Lord.

When you cultivate a joyful spirit, you are unable to be drowned in human emotion. Grief, sorrow, rage, and depression may still come, but these harrowing emotions will not be able to take control and rule the mind of a person who is truly joyful. When you allow joy from God into your heart, you find the ability to commandeer the emotions that used to control you.

I mean come on, how awesome is that?!

The Joyful Room

In our house, I have a room that is my very own. Not really an actual room, with a door and all, but a space in our home that has been dedicated to my creativity.

My husband and I both work from home and while he has an office upstairs, I felt the desire to have a designated area for myself where I could feel comfortable just being me.

Thus, we converted our formal dining room into the feng shui room. Although, we have since abolished the name because of the connotations that come along with it. It is now titled my (drumroll please) Creativity Corner!

I remember looking into the plain white room, shaking my head and thinking, "This just won't do."

Let me explain, back when I was really struggling with my alcoholism (at the time I'm writing this, I'm 5 years sober and counting all thanks to the wonderful Lord!) I attended two different rehabs. Although separate facilities, their interior was much the same. Obtrusive white walls, little to no windows, and a muting offensive undertone of desolation that has taken me years to shake off.

Every time I see white walls, I am reminded of some of the worst low-points of my life. Therefore, my already creative and colorful personality has morphed into somewhat of an extreme maximalist. The more things going on the better!

For my depressing blank dining room, I devised a master plan to enhance comfort and encourage creativity. After explaining said eccentric plan to my husband, he looked at me like I was crazy.

Nonetheless, this artist had a vision and that design was going to come to fruition.

Different colored tapestries, in a slew of sizes and shapes were hung on the walls. My old music festival umbrellas were attached to the upper corners of the room. Multitudes of Christmas lights were draped around the perimeter of the space, my multicolored star paper lanterns were hung from the ceiling, and plants were dispersed throughout every surface. A rug exploding in color and patterns was purchased for my birthday and a $20 futon was attained off of Craigslist. My coveted record player, pastel pink typewriter, and antique marble chess set were proudly displayed on top of a dresser in the room whose drawers were filled to the brim with my journals, crafting supplies, and overabundance of used records. The overhead light was shut off, twinkling Christmas lights and lanterns turned on, and the warm pink glow from my salt rock lamps produced a calming and inviting vibe.

This room brings me joy.

It has since become the favorite room in the house. Jake spends every morning here in prayer and devotional, before I kick him out to his office because as we joke, he can't have both. Stella is always found lounging in here, stretched out peacefully over the entire futon (she is such a big girl) or mixing in with the kaleidoscope of colors on the rug. Even friends and guests who enter our home always comment on the magnificence of this room.

As my one friend exclaimed (please note she is a minimalist to my maximalist, so this was a big feat for her), "There is absolutely no rhyme or order, but for some reason it not only works but is comforting."

This room of mine, this overflowing of colors and shapes, with millions of things going on at once is an example of a few lessons that the Lord taught me not too long ago.

I used to attempt to be normal, to have matching colors, not too many things overcrowding the walls, textures that complement. Blah, blah, blah. Deep down, the artist inside of me was screaming, "BORING!" but the people-pleaser on the outside simply shushed her true self and continued along, muting the very things that made her unique.

God has since allowed me to find myself. To accept His love and also accept His intricate design of my soul. To deny the individual that God created you to be is an utmost insult to our Father. He did not create me to like empty walls and a simple aesthetic.

I was made to look at an empty space and see an opportunity.

God designed me to thrive in variety. He called me to accept the uniqueness that is tattooed on my heart. By learning to accept the love that God so freely promised me, I have found permission to accept myself, flaws and all.

Now I find joy not in where I blend in, but where I stand out. I have come to relish who I was created to be.

Instead of being ashamed of my quirks and differences, I have found the Lord encouraging me to explore and nurture the very things that I used to wish away. I was meant to swim in a sea of rainbow, to thrive in a world of varying texture.

God did not create me to be like everyone else, or to even be like anyone else! I am special, thus I should allow myself to revel in the very things that make me distinct.

This room, that I am currently typing away in, is a very testament to that fact. It's the first room you lay eyes on when you walk through the front door, and while the old me might have fretted over what others would think, the beloved daughter of Christ prevailed and said, "Who cares!"

God created me to also be a creator. To tend to and care for the garden inside of myself. In order for my writing, my God-given purpose to blossom and grow, I have to allow myself to find joy in the things I was designed to be joyful in.

Ladies, we are all special. I am no more special than you are. God created each and every one of us to be different in our own ways. It's not wrong if you prefer minimal and unfussy designs, because that's what you were made to like!

But it is wrong for you to deny yourself an innocent opportunity to find joy in something. God wants us to be joyful. The more joy we allow into our hearts, the more joy we will have to give out and bestow on others.

"Now may the God of hope fill you with all joy and peace as you believe in Him so that you may overflow with hope by the power of the Holy Spirit." (Romans 15:13 HCSB)

You cannot pour from an empty cup. In order to spread light and love into this world, such as Jesus has commanded us to do, we need to fill our spiritual cup up.

In a world full of hate, we must learn to find joy, because joy leads to love and God is love.

Choose It, Don't Feel It

Every day I try to start my day with joy. By nature, I am not a morning person. Many times, I have a tendency to be grumpy and frumpy in the wee beginning hours of the day. Little things like my coffee getting cold or running out of ice for my water, used to set me off. But the Lord has commanded me to be joyful, so now every morning before I even get out of bed or check my phone, I thank the Lord for another day here on Earth to do the good work He has set before me. I rejoice in His gift of life for both myself and my family.

I choose joy.

In order to walk into the shoes laid out for each of us, we must learn to choose joy. To find the silver lining, so to speak. We are designed to flow in our Father's love, and with that obedience, there is much joy.

We must find reasons to be joyful, even in a seemingly joyless situation.

Take COVID-19 for example. Many people became ill, jobs were lost (mine included), lives were disrupted, and the entire economy took a major hit. There was so much fear being projectile vomited into the world. A very desolate and joyless situation, to say the least.

> *"Dear brothers and sisters, when troubles of any kind come your way, consider it an opportunity for great joy. For you know that when your faith is tested, your endurance has a chance to grow." (James 1:2-3 NLT)*

As believers we are called to find the joy, no matter the circumstances. So my husband and I decided to relish in the fact that we were able to spend more quality time together. We found joy in realizing that we needed to increase our prayer lives and spend more time with the Lord on a daily basis, to make sure to put on our God armor during such an uncertain time. I chose to find joy in the opportunity that I now had at being able to enhance my cooking skills because of more free time.

It was not always easy, and sometimes it was downright forced. But by continually setting out to have a joyful heart, eventually the feeling came naturally and I was able to feel the Lord lifting weight off my shoulders. Do not stop flowing in God's purpose and authority for your life.

Never stop seeking to uncover the joy.

There is nothing more ravishing than a joyful heart. We were called to be joyful, not only to rejoice in the Lord, but to rejoice in the blessings and gifts He has bestowed upon us.

Please try and be purposeful with cultivating a joyful heart. Life will forever be filled with ups and downs, unexpected frustrations, and sudden tragedies. Our life here on Earth is not meant to be all peaches and cream, but by learning to find joy in the simple things… in the light breeze, the wind kissing your face, or the baby who smiles at you amidst the grocery store aisle.

There are moments for joy all around us, we just have to ask the Holy Spirit to open us up to interpreting them.

One thing that really helped my husband and I to train and cultivate a naturally joyful heart, was that we were purposeful on both starting and ending each day with joy. Every night before bed we say three things each that we are grateful for. Not every day is going to have this grandiose list, but sometimes just simply saying I am grateful for having shelter and a warm place to lay my head helps to reposition your heart.

Finding gratefulness in even the humble things, helps to encourage you to nurture the joy inside of your soul.

By thanking the Lord for another day as soon as you open your eyes, you will start your day with a joyful mindset. Begin your morning from a place of gratitude as many people don't get another chance to wake up. Always remember that our time here is limited.

Find the joy in realizing that you have been given another opportunity to fulfill the purpose that God has created for you. Hallelujah!

I challenge you to find the joy in your life by beginning and ending each day with gratitude. Grab ahold of joy tightly and never let it go.

The Healing Tears

I'm a crier. Like, big time.

Back when I was all hollow and empty, I rarely cried. I shoved my emotions so far down, trying not to recognize them, and most definitely not wanting to feel them. And then one day, I told my testimony to a new counselor and she looked at me, with tears shining in her own eyes and asked, "Do you not feel the weight of your own story? You just told it like you were telling me about the weather."

I didn't really know what to say to that. I knew the facts to my story, and I had learned to recite them almost robotically. But actually allowing myself to feel it?

Nuh uh, no way. That was too much for me.

This very counselor helped me to stop dissociating and understand that it's okay to cry. It doesn't make you weak, but it allows you to get out some pent up frustration, hurt, or just pressing emotion.

Once I learned that it was okay to cry, and broke the seal on that bodily function. The floodgates to an overfilled dam were ruptured. I cried and cried and cried. I cried when I was sad and depressed. I cried when I was angry and frustrated. I even cried when I was happy.

I was so confused!

I used to be ashamed of my tears. Once I allowed them to be a part of my life, they were always there. But now I recognize that God created me to be a person who experiences deep intense emotions, whether that be intensely ecstatic or intensely melancholy.

Heck, I even cry during movies now. I can be watching a Disney Princess movie and I'll shed a few tears at the happily ever after that takes place!

Gah!

However I have learned a valuable lesson through this. That sometimes we just need to cry out to God.

Sometimes we need to let it all out. Let our sorrows go, release them, and get them out of our bodies. It is very true when women are compared to ovens. Sometimes I just let something simmer, and eventually I forget what all I have thrown into my heated pot until it boils over and explodes out. Yuck.

We weren't created to always contain our emotions. We have feelings for a reason, and sometimes the best way to deal with them is by letting them out!

By no means should we do this in inappropriate manners, so please understand where I am going with this. I don't want you to bite your mother-in-law's head off and say I suggested it. But I do think sometimes you just need a good cry. And not the pretty kind where you still look all beautiful except for the fact that your eyelashes are glistening with tears.

I mean seriously, who actually cries like that?

No sweet sister, just cry. Let it all out. Give that pain, frustration, sorrow, rejection, confusion, and rage to God. He can handle it, but we cannot. It's okay for your face to get puffy, snot to run down your nose, and your eyes to swell up.

This is a no-judgement zone here.

When I first started to allow myself to cry, I used to judge the way I did it. No lie, I would look in the mirror and try to determine if I was a pretty crier. If I could cry, but somehow not look like a monstrosity while doing it, then I felt like it was a success.

I know, how silly is that?!

The whole point of crying is to let go. To stop holding on to the emotion that you just can't take anymore.

Now, I don't like to look at myself when I cry. I either try and do it in a dark place, where I can ask Jesus to take my weary heart in His hands. Or I do it in the shower. I plop my naked self down in my shower, with the hot water running over me and bawl like a baby.

I can be as loud as I want, the shower usually masks it and I just give my pain to God. I cry to my Father, and beg Him to help me. To guide me on whatever problem is causing me angst.

And I'll tell ya. Typically, after a good cry, bringing my issues to Jesus, really makes me feel better. Sometimes I receive insight during that time of being vulnerable about what direction I should go with said issue. Or other times I just feel lighter, that the simple act of crying out to my Creator really helps to lessen my burden.

Yes, a hardcore cry sesh will make you tired, face a little puffy, and you might have a slight headache, but overall you will feel better! You will feel a sense of relief; the tension of the issue isn't boiling over inside of you any longer.

Now why am I talking about crying during this chapter titled Joy you may ask?

Because joy is meant not to be an emotional experience, but a state of living. A homeostasis for your life.

Joy should be your neutral, and although that is easier said than done, it is so important to recognize that although a lot of bad things can be going on in your life, your heart, and your mind, you can still project joy in the midst of a burden.

When I cry out to God, in that moment I may feel an intense unpleasant emotion, but my heart is still remaining ultimately joyful. I can be told the lie that my life sucks, and in the moment fall into believing that temptation, but in my heart I know that I am saved. That I am loved and that my life is a blessing, each and every day that I get to spend here on this Earth.

The Hubz and I could be in a petty argument, and in the moment, I could feel dissatisfied in our marital communication, but in my heart I still hold joy. Because I know that Our Heavenly Father created us for one another. That my spouse was made for me, and me alone. That in our hearts we will always love one another, and although in the heat of the moment we both might be a little stubborn, that our God always calls us to come together and love with His perfect love.

If your joy comes from God, then it can never be stolen away by a measly human or worldly event. The joy you have will come supercharged straight from Heaven.

Be Joyful Like Jesus

Jesus was a very joyful man. There were many things that brought Him joy, yet these things were not actually tangible items at all. Material possessions were not what brought Jesus joy. No, it was obedience to the Father that made Him the happiest.

In Luke 10:21 it says that, "Jesus was full of joy through the Holy Spirit."

Our joy is not meant to be produced from anything within this world. We will not find true joy from shopping, traveling, or losing weight. Real joy will come from within, not as a result of your extenuating circumstances.

Jesus was able to become full of joy from within, by tapping into the power source of the Holy Spirit. This is where our joy is located too. The real joy of your life will be provided to you through your Heavenly Father, who delights in your joyfulness!

> *"I pray that God, the source of hope, will fill you completely with joy and peace because you trust in him. Then you will overflow with confident hope through the power of the Holy Spirit." (Romans 15:13 NLT)*

Although it seems impossible, joy that comes from the Spirit is evident even in the midst of tragedy. During a time of devastation and loss, joy can still be found through God. This type of joy is unable to be tampered with, as it triumphs and endures even the worst of circumstances.

God wants His children to be joyful. He wants us to smile, laugh, and be merry. He created joy for this very reason and desires for us to experience it to the fullest!

Saved followers are meant to rejoice! We are created to find joy in our all-loving Lord, joy in one another, joy in God's Word, joy in our worship, and joy in even the simplest aspects of our lives.

Happiness may be a fleeting feeling but joy is a steady state of being. You see, happiness is what happens to you, while joy is what happens within you.

Choose joy.

I believe the opposite of being joyful is being jaded. And let me tell you, I used to be a very jaded person. I used to focus on all of the wrong going on in the world, instead of the areas of success within the Kingdom.

The cup wasn't even half empty to me, there was no liquid in it at all!

Happy versus sad, is such a bland and blanketed term of expression. These two words are just meaningless feelings, fleeting in whatever circumstance you are experiencing. But being joyful versus jaded is much different. These are places of residing. This is choosing to either remain in a positive state of being or negative. These are not simple emotions here one second and gone the next. They are places where you plant your heart and allow roots to grow.

Have you ever stopped to contemplate the difference between happiness and joy? At first, I believed these were just synonyms describing the same emotion. I have come to find that happiness is a human made feeling, while joy is a holy one.

Happiness is fickle, comes easily and departs just as quickly. While joy is much different. Joy is not an emotion, but instead a place of residing.

Think of a life raft inside a raging storm. The waves may crash against it, but it will not capsize. You will remain anchored to its safety and refuge as long as the Father wills it.

I have fallen victim to being a victim. Victimizing myself and my misfortunes. I used to focus on all of the things that were going wrong in my life, rather than counting my numerous blessings. I don't want you to make the same mistake that I made, allowing myself to live in a jaded state.

Thus, I challenge you today to make a list of at least 10 occurrences in your life that bring you joy. Not happiness, like the feeling those cute bellbottoms you found at the thrift shop the other day provided. But moments in your life that God allowed you to experience utter joy.

I have done this challenge myself, and what I have found is that the moments of my life that were the most joyful were instances that I could very clearly discern the hand of God working.

The world is not always a joyful place, but God can always give you joy within this world. We need to thank God for all of the relationships and instances in our lives that we have been able to feel His inexpressible joy. This joy is beautiful and worthy of our appreciation, God so deserving of our praise.

Peace is finding solace and rest in the assurance of God's promises.

Peace

I have a magnet on my fridge that I've had since college. It has remained anchored to my many fridges since then and through a multitude of moves I have always made sure to put it back up.

It reads, "Peace. It does not mean to be in a place where there is no noise, trouble or hard work. It means to be in the midst of those things and still be calm in your heart."

You see, peace is finding solace and rest in the assurance of God's promises. It is having utmost confidence that our Lord is who He claims to be and knowing that He will care for you, His beloved child.

Peaceful people refrain from going to war with their actions or thoughts, as they recognize that no solution can be wrought through these harmful manners. When you choose to work towards a common goal, instead of insisting things be done your way, you are enacting peace.

A great example of this is an ongoing joke that my husband and I have. Whenever we face a situation, whether it be as simple as walking to the peanut butter aisle or more serious like picking out our new family vehicle to purchase, we always go in totally opposite directions. Both in the physical and metaphorical sense, yet somehow end up at the same solution every single time.

He will go to the left side of the grocery store to get to the peanut butter aisle and I will go from the right side. He will research cars on Carfax and then only want to go look at the vehicles that meet his criteria, while I like to go test drive actual vehicles at the different car lots and research the ones I like in between car appointments. We always end up at the same spot at the same time, or come to the same conclusion as to which vehicle is best for our family, but we consistently approach a problem from different angles.

Early in our marriage, this would cause quite a few tiffs. As we both like to believe we are right most of the time. And the funny thing was that we were both agreeing on whatever the situation solution was, we just wanted to go about it in varying manners.

The Lord has had to teach me peace in this area. To pick my battles and to know when to hold my tongue. Now, instead of having a "my way or the highway" mindset, Jake and I approach problems as teammates, listen to the others opinion on the matter, and work together to find an appropriate solution.

Hold Tight To Peace

Today, coincidentally as I am working on this chapter I am having a very hard time getting into a peaceful state of mind. My husband has decided today of all days he wants to act like a mischievous little boy by tickling, poking, and walking by me for the sole purpose of pushing random buttons on my keyboard. There is roof construction going on outside that is loud and noisy and on top of that all I'm pretty positive there is a crow stuck in our chimney, and flapping frantically about.

I grumpily moved from my creative corner to the living room because the commotion outside was causing a headache and now there is such a banging going on inside my chimney that I feel somewhat in a state of distress.

Shouting for Jake to come downstairs and help me investigate the possibly trapped crow situation. My husband assured me from the banister that I was hearing things. So I put on some loud smooth jazz, turned on my essential oil diffuser, made myself a steaming hot cup of espresso, settling down once more, trying to create the perfect serene moment to dive into this chapter.

All of a sudden, like a car alarm going off, the loudest "CAW, CAW, CAW!" sounded from inside my fireplace. I frantically forced my husband to come downstairs, as now I'm convinced there is a black monstrosity inside of our chimney!

You see, the crows here in Oregon are as big as my 18-pound cat. They are gigantic and bully all of the smaller animals around. Even on my evening walks, I have been harassed by a territorial crow once or twice.

I attempted to persuade Jake to inspect the opening in our fireplace, to which he absolutely refused. Begrudgingly, I got down on my hands and knees, lifted my iPhone shakily with the flashlight app shining and put my head inside of the soot filled fireplace, not knowing what I was going to find.

My husband, being the jokester that he is, decided this was a great opportunity and the perfect moment to tap my bum with his foot. I screamed like a pterodactyl, the crow angrily retorted, and Jake laughed hysterically.

Needless to say we have since called someone to further investigate, my smooth jazz is blasting at a very obnoxious level, and I am attempting to get back to a peaceful center.

I can't help but internally chuckle, as maybe this is the exact story God wanted me to experience when writing this chapter. Life isn't perfect, and although there are great moments that feel heavenly, that fleeting instance is definitely the exception not the rule.

Most of the time, life is messy, chaotic, and just downright laughable.

Peace, as I am continually taught, is not found. It is felt. Peace that comes from within is so much better than peace that is produced from our outside surroundings. Yes, it would totally be awesome to have both, but sometimes life is just difficult.

Heck, my blog is even titled, "The Happy Hot Mess" because that is what I am! I am trying to navigate happiness, and peace of spirit in the midst of chaos. I am a hot mess express, my coffee is most often spilt, and my socks rarely match.

But that's okay, because God called me to be peaceful, not perfect.

I feel like many of us fall into the trap of thinking we have to be this pristine version of ourselves. That in order for God to use us we need to have money, status, a platform, and so forth. That we can't still be in the midst of a struggle in order for God to use us to spread His teachings.

This is so untrue, just think about Jesus's disciples. None of them were in the best position, but that didn't make a difference to Jesus. He was able to use them and find their value even in the midst of their messiness.

The only thing we truly need in order to let God use us as an instrument for His divine purposes is to allow His peace to surpass everything and reside in our hearts always.

I used to let every little thing bother me. I had zero tolerance for stress. I have struggled quite a bit with anxiety throughout my lifetime. I would think out every decision in my life 15 million steps ahead, allow thousands of what-ifs to course through my mind, and cripple myself mentally from situations before they ever came to pass.

Two Bible verses really helped to ground me, and allowed me to feel a sense of peace

> *"Therefore don't worry about tomorrow, because tomorrow will worry about itself. Each day has enough trouble of its own."*
> *(Matthew 6:34 HCSB)*

"Don't worry about anything, but in everything, through prayer and petition with thanksgiving, let your requests be made known to God. And the peace of God, which surpasses every thought, will guard your hearts and minds in Christ Jesus." (Philippians 4:6-8 HCSB)

Grasping The Peace Of Jesus

"Peace does not come because you finally have control over your life; peace comes when you no longer need control." – Erwin Raphael McManus

Try not to let your heart be troubled. God wants to shape your identity, and blossom His everlasting peace throughout your life.

Jesus allowed internal peace from the Spirit to lead His life. Although His life on Earth was anything but peaceful, Jesus walked with the Holy Spirit guiding His steps. He didn't allow the attacks of the enemy to sway His peaceful homeostasis.

Jesus shared His peace with everyone who would grasp onto it. That's why He gave us the Holy Spirit, so that we could have a direct connection to our Heavenly Father and the calming refuge that He provides. By cultivating your relationship with God, one day you will find that even in the midst of danger you can be peaceful at heart.

"I have told you all this so that you may have peace in me. Here on Earth you will have many trials and sorrows. But take heart, because I have overcome the world." (John 16:33 NLT)

We must be diligent in doing the work that the Lord has set out before us. We must have peace to walk fearlessly through wherever God is willing us to go. We must open our arms to all of God's children, even the ones that we would much rather love from afar.

I have personally felt the assuring embrace of Jesus wrapping His arms around my soul. We are sheltered in Christ's love, protected by His Spirit, and soothed by His unworldly peace. This peace is given to us through the Holy Spirit, a peace that is never lacking or desolate. A peace that can blanket the Earth, and be shared with all.

This peace will not run out; everyone gets their fair share.

In this world we live in, there will undoubtedly be trouble. But we each can rest assured knowing that the Prince of Peace is lobbying for us, ruling over our naturally fearful hearts. Through His Spirit, we are able to face even the worst situation with grace, faith, and composure.

> *"Peace I leave with you. My peace I give to you. I do not give to you as the world gives. Your heart must not be troubled or fearful." (John 14:27 HCSB)*

Peace is an often thrown around word. A whole movement of hippies used the peace symbol as their logo. Many people talk about peace, but how many do you think actually experience it?

I encourage you to be a peacekeeper, to make the conscious decision to spread peace wherever you go and with whoever you interact with today. When you choose peace over conflict, and go to God with all of your worries, watch and see what miraculous things happen.

Choose God instead of stress and ask Him to help you experience peace in every area of your life.

> *"Don't worry about anything, but in everything, through prayer and petition with thanksgiving, let your requests be made known to God. And the peace of God, which surpasses every thought, will guard your hearts and minds in Christ Jesus." (Philippians 4:6-7 HCSB)*

Persevering In Peace

I used to live of the world, with a sinful self-serving outlook on life. Let's be honest, the world is a pretty dark place. There is so much corruption, greed, death, and destruction. Wars are continuously being waged, children are being used as sex slaves, money has become an idol, the list goes on and on. By staying stuck in the mindset of the world, I was mentally ill. But once I acknowledged and embraced that I was a citizen of Heaven, only residing in the world temporarily, my struggle with anxiety became a heck of a lot easier.

> *"For the mind-set of the flesh is death, but the mind-set of the Spirit is life and peace." (Romans 8:6 HCSB)*

No, my anxiety has not altogether disappeared, there are still better days than others. But my foundation is solid, no longer shaky and crumbling. The Lord is my Father, and I am His prized child. He sent His one and only Son to die for my sins.

What an honor! And He has blessed me with the Holy Spirit dwelling inside of myself, guiding me towards the light.

The enemy has nothing on the Holy Trinity! I have peace in my heart knowing that I am on the winning side of a spiritual battle that is being waged right as we speak.

I was created to be a Warrior Princess for my King. My weapons are that of love and mercy, my infantry fights for peace. Although the message is love, sometimes we have to fight for that love. It is important to remember that Jesus was both the lamb, and the lion.

True peace is only attainable through perseverance.

So I challenge you, sweet friend, to find peace in your soul. To ask God to aid you in staying peaceful at heart. To try and not let the world bring you down, but to instead let some of that unearthly beauty inside of you to shine out onto those you interact with.

Allow God to use you to be a light in this dark world. Let your problems become less and your God become more. That is the way to enable peace to pervade every part of your being.

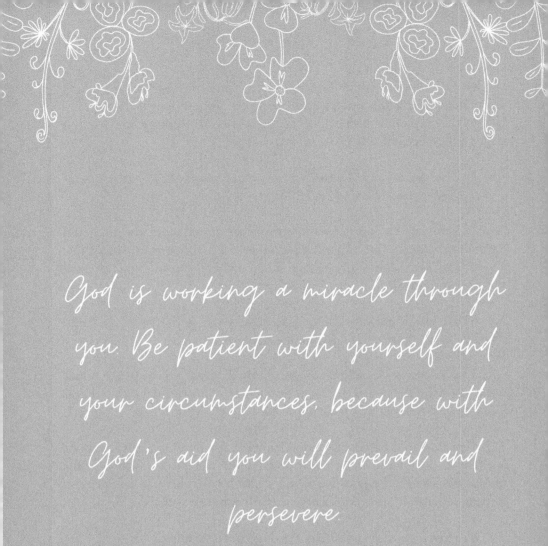

God is working a miracle through you. Be patient with yourself and your circumstances, because with God's aid you will prevail and persevere.

Patience

Patience is exhibiting a calm demeanor in the midst of a stressful circumstance. It is not overreacting, becoming easily annoyed, or irritated.

Patient people handle a difficult situation with grace, able to expertly discern if an issue is worth getting disgruntled over. While staying collected and picking their battles wisely, they are able to distinguish between what matters only in the moment and what will have future implications.

Supporting the growth and journey of others produces patience. When we bestow tolerance and empathy to a difficult person, rather than giving them a piece of our mind, we are watering the roots of patience.

So with that in mind, what areas of your life do you have the most patience? And the least?

Healthy Healing

If there was one aspect of the Fruit of the Spirit that I continually struggle with, this one is it.

I have never been the most patient person. I don't do puzzles, because they take too long and make me frustrated. Monopoly is my least favorite game because it drags on for hours. Ironically it's also my husband's favorite board game, so I'm attempting to work through that.

Like a spoiled child, when I want something– I want it now. But what God is continually showing me, teaching me over and over, is that great things take time. Success doesn't happen overnight. Dreams don't come true in the blink of an eye. And patience is one of the most important aspects of the Fruit of the Spirit to embrace if you plan on living a content life.

I used to struggle a lot with my self-image, and admittedly I could still be better at it. I've never been an especially thin and lean body type. I am above average height and the Lord blessed me with some curves. Growing up, I always envied the petite girls who could fit into a 0 or bless their hearts 00.

That was never me.

From a very young age, I learned how to count calories. I knew what cellulite was and I obsessed over what that silly number on the scale said. It defined me.

It got to the point where I developed an unhealthy relationship with food, either not eating or binge gorging my feelings on junk food when my emotions got out of control. It took a very long time for me to learn a healthy medium, where I was both properly nourished yet not overstuffed.

My family was never made aware of this struggle because in truth there were many other more pressing aspects of my life that needed to be dealt with. Some of my sins were as ugly and obtrusive as a large pus-filled zit on your chin, painstakingly obvious to the entire world, while others could slide by undetected.

I tried many fad diets, including the no eating until you pass out one. Some worked for a short while, but in the end, I always gained the weight back. I have no doubt that I truly messed my metabolism up royally, and now I get sad just thinking about the destruction I purposefully did to my poor body.

Sometimes I just wish I could go back and hug my teenage self. To stroke her hair, let her sob on my shoulder, and tell her that she will make it. That she has a Father who loves her more than she can even comprehend. That she just needs to be patient with herself and her circumstances, because with God's aid she will prevail and persevere.

Be patient with the process of your growth.

Your entire life will be filled with mountains and valleys. But I'll tell ya one thing, the glorious mountain top moments of my life way overpower the dark low valley points.

I have always struggled with patience. When I wanted to be fit and *skinny* (I despise that word now), I was willing to do anything to get that instant gratification. You name it, I probably tried it. But the results were fake, faulty, and not lasting. It's like our walk with the Lord. The first step is of course, accepting that Jesus died on the cross for your sins. But you can't just pop that pill and expect everything in life to get miraculously better.

You have to actively walk out the Lord's purpose for you with Him. It's imperative to dedicate and discipline yourself to regularly get into God's Living Word through the Bible. You must learn to train and fine-tune your ears to listen to the Holy Spirit working through you, speaking words of advice and guidance to you.

There is no quick fix to being a "good" Christian.

I had to learn this the hard way regarding both my physical health, and my spiritual health. In order to lose fat (I try to no longer give power to the number on the scale) I needed to have a full lifestyle overhaul.

No more pouring half a cup full of my hazelnut Coffeemate creamer into my cup. I switched it for almond milk flavored hazelnut creamer, then I moved to just a splash of unsweetened almond milk, and now I drink my coffee black and enjoy it more this way than I ever did before.

Who would have thought?! But, do you see the process that had to occur in order for a habit to stick?

I used to be an all or nothing girl. If I was going to do something, then there was no half-hineying it. I was going all out. Go big or go home was an immature motto I wholeheartedly adopted.

In my past, if I was going to do something, then I was going full force, like when I decided I wanted to get into boxing so I joined an actual boxing league with no prior experience.

The team had to train for 10 hours a week at a pro boxing gym, amidst the slums of south Austin. I was pushed to my very limit, leaving each gym session with my legs barely able to hold my sweat-soaked self up. Every person on the team had hulking muscles in places I didn't even realize could be buff. My family all cautioned me that this was yet another one of my horrible ideas, but I was determined to be the next female Rocky.

The time came for me to spar in the cage. The other trainers and teammates were yelling and shaking the fenced octagon ring, amping up the intensity of the match with their volume. My heart was racing as I squared up against my opponent, a massive man and ex professional boxer. My adrenaline spiked as the bell rang, signaling the beginning of the round.

I ducked and dodged, blow after blow, but the fighter kept mercilessly coming at me. I danced around the ring trying to protect myself from his combination of powerful punches. Although I was on the defensive, I kept trying to fight back, my punches falling short.

The hungry fighter advanced on me and threw a devastatingly powerful left hook… and I dopped like a sack of potatoes. I was down and out.

Inevitably, my tooth was chipped along with my imaginary bravado and confidence.

Ya'll, I burnt out HARD.

In the upcoming month I was supposed to compete against the Denver boxing league, but my shaking arms could barely hold up my gloves. I was afraid of virtually every swole person on the team and after my tooth got chipped both my pride and my dignity were damaged along with it.

It's not my proudest moment to say that I quit. I ran away like a scared little puppy, and no longer had a desire to box.

What is the moral of this ridiculous, yet also kind of hilarious story? That although I had good initial intentions for wanting to box, such as getting healthier while also doing something I had a general interest in, I did not go about it in the right way. I went way overboard, which ultimately led to my burnout. I should have just taken a few classes a week at Title Boxing and worked my way up if I wanted to get more involved. Then I would have been able to stick with it, increasing my boxing endurance along the way and would not have gotten injured.

I have had to learn this burnout lesson more than a few times, and I have finally begun to apply the principle of incremental changes to my life in virtually every aspect.

If I wanted to be healthy and toned, then I needed to stop looking for a quick fix. I needed to begin to take small steps and start working out regularly. And not the kind of workout you do until you throw up, but start with something easy like power walking on an inclined treadmill and work my way up to those hardcore cycling classes with the flashing lights that make you feel like you're in a rave.

If I wanted to fix my relationship with food, then I had to stop thinking that it was either salad or multiple Crunch Wrap Supremes at Taco Bell. I needed to dedicate some time, energy, and patience towards learning my way around the kitchen and finding creative ways to intertwine veggies into basically every meal that I ate.

When I made the decision to stop eating meat, my blood pressure at the time was extremely high and I was on blood pressure medication that I wanted to get off of immediately. Through my degree plan at my college, Texas A&M, I learned the ins and outs of the agriculture industry. You see, I got my bachelor degree in Agricultural Communications and Journalism, so that I could be better informed on how to live the healthiest life possible and how to best take care of our environment while doing it.

However, ironically everything that I learned about our food industry and the way in which our meat is produced ultimately led to my decision to not eat it anymore. I'm a native Texan, and we like our BBQ, fajitas, and carne asada. Meat was a staple in all 3 meals I ate each day.

Trying to avoid my typical burnout pattern, I made the educated simple decision to cut meat down to only one meal a day at first. And I began to feel so much more energy during breakfast and lunch than I did during dinner time when I had my meat meal. So then I decided to just do a little experiment on myself and only eat meat 3 days a week.

The difference that I felt both physically and emotionally was insane. I was in disbelief that just by simply not eating meat for 4 days out of the week I was able to feel this good. Finally, I decided to cut it all out. No more moist brisket and juicy ribs for me.

No kidding, my life transformed!

I was able to drop 25 pounds like it was nothing. I was able to get off my blood pressure medication, AND get off of my antidepressants. It was so unreal to me that a simple diet change could create such a difference in my life.

But the truth was, that it still took time and I had to be patient with the process.

I learned that just like a car needs gasoline to make it run smoothly, our bodies too need proper fuel. Your car is going to run a lot better and last a lot longer when you pay a bit extra and fill it regularly with premium gas. Our bodies are the same, by subbing out meat-dominant meals for plant-based meals my body began to run much better. Now, my plate every day is a fun creative challenge for me, to see if I can engineer a meal where I can indeed taste and see the rainbow with every bite!

Now, I eat my veggies regularly. I'm not afraid of trying a new healthy food, like roasted seaweed or dragon fruit. I have even titled myself the Mad Scientist in the kitchen!

Who would have thought!?

However, I also make awesome vegan homemade versions of my old friend, the Crunch Wrap Supreme. I have found a healthy moderation between being too hardcore and cutting things cold-turkey versus learning when it is okay to indulge. I workout between 3-5 times a week and sometimes I do yoga, sometimes a stationary bike, and other times I crank it hard on the stair stepper with weights.

It's all about balance and patience with the process. My health is a long-term commitment towards making good choices and being informed about the best ways to care for the temple that God has given me.

This is the mindset we should also have in regards to our faith. Yes, it would be awesome if every day you could read the Bible for an hour, do a devotional, listen to a sermon, spend time solely devoted in prayer, write to the Lord, and have worship music playing as constant elevator music to your life.

But get real, that's just not possible!

If you tried to do all that, I bet you would burnout hardcore. God doesn't expect you to become as great as Moses overnight. He wants to grow and cultivate you in stages.

Much like the butterfly, you will experience growing in different aspects of your life at different times.

It's all about building healthy spiritual habits and finding realistic ways to walk out your faith every day. Some days I wake up, read the Bible, do a devotional, and write to the Lord in my morning pages. Other days I blast worship music while getting ready and pray while driving to an appointment. And some days I am simply worn out and find myself listening to a sermon while doing the dishes (my least favorite chore in the world).

It's all about balance and moderation.

In my early walk with the Lord, I thought in order for God to hear me I had to be in a formal setting of prayer. I needed to be on my knees (which always hurt me because my knees have never been the best) and be in a peaceful quiet place and speak to the Lord in a formal manner that did not feel like me.

But now I recognize that God wants to have a real relationship with us. We can pray to him all throughout the day! We can pray to him when we wake up, when we are stuck in line at the grocery store, and when we are in a petty argument with our family over something unimportant.

God wants to be an active part of our lives, so we need to be purposeful in making it so.

Yes, it's important to cultivate a habit of dedicating time every day to the Lord, but it's also important to realize that life happens. Your alarm doesn't go off and you're late dropping the kids off to school, so you have to forgo your morning devotional. You get sick and can't make it to church. You have a work holiday party and have to miss your sisterhood meeting. It's okay! God is patient with His children and we need to learn to be patient with ourselves too.

In an unpredictable world, the only thing we can truly rely on is God.

Instead of resisting and wishing away the struggle at hand, what if we learned to cherish and embrace it?

Housewife Barbie

Some days I just feel tired. Take yesterday for example. I woke up around 9 am, bopped around until 2 pm when I could no longer even keep my eyes open. Took an hour snoozer and then somehow still passed out after dinner at 7 pm. I just woke up and it is 8:30 am.

Man, was I tired!

Do you ever have days like that? Days where you know you should be working, writing, cleaning, running errands or so forth and all you can manage to do is sleep for most of the day?

I used to get really down on myself for these unproductive days. I used to bully myself internally and try to make up for my lack of productivity by doing double the next day. It would just snowball effect every day until eventually my to-do list was over 30 things long and I was constantly running around in a million different directions. Then enter the tired day again, when my mind was fried and my body was uncooperative.

Have you ever found yourself in a similar cycle?

One thing that God has revealed to me over the past couple of years is my busyness. He has shown me that although my ambitions come from the right place, I can mistake my initiative and use its momentum in the wrong ways.

How many times in a day do you use the word busy or stressed? I know personally, at least a couple!

How busy we are is a direct indicator of how closely we are walking with God. No, I don't mean to say that just because you're busy you're not a good Christian. That's not the point I'm trying to make. But by staying in a constant state of "busy" we are robbing Jesus of the opportunity to dwell with us in our silence. We need to learn to put the to-do list aside every now and then and simply be still with God. There needs to be a balance of both in our lives.

I remember a time when my to-do list ruled my life. What started out as a good habit, quickly became a debilitating obsession. Side note: addiction does not just come in the form of drugs and alcohol; busyness can indeed be an addiction.

I would get so frazzled if my never-ending to-do list wasn't completed. And then on the off chance that I actually did complete my 50 bullet-point checklist I still wouldn't allow myself to feel accomplished of the hard work that I had put in that day. Because in my mind, if I was able to complete all my tasks then they must not have been hard enough to begin with.

This cycle went on for a very long time, and I even began to value my seemingly all-important to-do list over allocating quality time with the valuable relationships in my life and even God himself.

My endless answer to how I was doing automatically came out as, "Man, I'm just so busy and stressed."

But the funny part was, that I myself was causing most of my stress by trying to hold myself to such an unrealistically high standard! Raise your hand if you realize that you too might be doing this to yourself.

It's not a priority to clean out your storage closet, even though deep down you would feel a lot better if you did. It's not a priority to organize your iPhone photos into specific categories and trips, even though you would love it if you were able to. And it's totally not a priority to sort your closet by shirt type and dress length, because even though you would aesthetically appreciate the ease of dressing every day, you should use that time to have a quality Bible study with your husband and make a nice healthy home-cooked meal.

But wait Madison, aren't all of those above things good things to do?!

I know, I was confused too. YES. All of the above to-do list tasks are good things to do, but not all in one day and surely not in replacement of quality time with God and your loved ones.

You see, God wants there to be a balance in your life, in correlation with all the things that you do. He wants you to be able to be a functioning adult who works and makes a living, so that you can provide and survive for your family. Yet, he also wants you to thrive within a healthy active God-community, serve others in need, and spend quality time with Him and His Son daily.

God does not want you to have a disproportionate relationship with the responsibilities in your life.

At the very start of Jake and I's marriage I struggled with this understanding quite a bit. I assumed that since I was now adopting the brand new title of "wife" that I needed to work off my little tail feathers being all domesticated and house-wifey. This was very hard for me at first because I am quite the free-spirit, so I was struggling with adopting a normal serving attitude towards my husband and our household maintenance.

I cooked 3 home-cooked meals a day, I deep cleaned everything with a weekly cleaning schedule, I dressed up nicely, I grocery shopped and tried very hard to make the holidays super exciting by decorating every square inch of our home, making full on Thanksgiving and Christmas meals all by myself for just the two of us, and throwing festive holiday parties.

Our house looked great, we were fed like we had a personal chef, the holiday parties made life-long jolly memories… and I was utterly exhausted. Like dead on my feet tired, if you looked at me the wrong way I might burst into tears overwhelmed. I was so busy trying to be who I thought I should be, adopting this new title for my life with overenthusiasm and gusto, that I was unintentionally robbing myself of some of the very things I needed in order to thrive.

I needed my daily God time in order to fill up my spiritual cup, because in all honesty during that season of our marriage I was pouring from empty. Which was rendering me utterly depleted. I needed my writing time, because when I do not write I'm not able to be who I was created to be. I need to write in order to process my feelings and understand some of the things that God was working through me. And I needed my alone time. By serving constantly, I was becoming very cranky. As an extroverted introvert, I can thrive with others and be absolutely fine, but then I need to decompress. By not giving myself the alone-time that I required after serving others all day or being around big groups of people regularly, I was just a ticking time bomb waiting to randomly detonate.

And detonate I did.

Jake and I got married at the start of Fall. So I rushed into the holidays full-force as new-wife Barbie. And I'll admit, I was on fire. But by the time Christmas was coming around I was starting to feel more than a little exhausted. A little less pep in my step, and a little more wanting to take a vacation away from everyone so that I could have a day in silence to drink my hot coffee, read my daily devotional, and write my little heart out.

As I have mentioned before, I have an already unnaturally large family. Even pre-marriage the Christmas parties were never-ending and although they're great fun, they are also tiring for someone who gets drained by social gatherings. However, this year was different, because we also added in church Christmas gatherings, friend holiday parties, and all of my husband's wonderful family events.

I bet you are rolling your eyes right now; I know sometimes I do sound kind of bratty. Jake and I are immensely blessed with community and I love his family and all of the people we have collectively added into our circle. But I was also not properly communicating my need for some decompress self-care time after each of these events and thus went on serving and pretending like I wasn't frazzled on the inside.

Our first married Christmas together was wonderful, nothing could ever take that away. But at 11:45 pm on Christmas evening while still at our 11th (yes I counted and it was really 11) Christmas gathering continued, I lost it.

At this time, I had separated myself from the masses and was sitting outside on the patio, trying to take deep breaths to hold the impending tears at bay. I was done, absolutely spent. I was so utterly exhausted, my face hurt from smiling, and all I wanted to do was crawl into bed and nap for a month.

Since our wedding madness, planning both an Italian elopement and a traditional Texas wedding ceremony in less than four months' time. After loving on everyone that attended our ceremony and reception, I had really not had any downtime. We moved into an apartment in downtown Austin, I started a new position as a realtor and my cystic acne came back with a vengeance from all the stress.

I had been so busy wrapped up in the unrealistic expectation that I needed to be a perfect wife that I was failing at being a dedicated Christian. I had been slacking on my God time, because typically I like to do my God time first thing in the morning with a hot cup of coffee. But since I had wholeheartedly adopted the role of personal chef and Jake woke up before me, by the time I got out of bed it was time for me to make him breakfast and by that point my untouched cup of coffee was cold and it was time for me to embark on the rest of my daily duties.

I very rarely wrote anymore, because my internal well was empty and I had nothing to pour out. And I was not communicating or giving myself the decompress alone time that I needed after each big event.

Jake came out all jolly and merry that late Christmas night to find his distraught and depleted new wife in tears. You see, my sweet Jake is an extrovert at heart. He thrives in the throngs of people, so it was hard for him to understand that I'm a very different creature. We have since taken personality tests and spiritual gift tests and been able to better understand how each other operates best.

The week after Christmas I came down with a nasty cold. I had utterly exhausted my body, to the point of sickness. The doctor ordered me to sleep that week and sleep is what I did. Jake had to make breakfast for himself, and we discovered that he is actually a breakfast king. That he rules the kitchen in the breakfast arena, and that he really enjoyed being able to dictate when and what he ate for breakfast every morning.

I was able to catch up on my Bible studies and God time, and I slowly felt my spiritual cup begin to fill up again. And boy let me tell ya, what a wonderful feeling that was!

And when invited to a New Years Eve Party, my husband looked lovingly at me and politely declined. Knowing that his wife just needed some peace and quiet to ring in the New Year, so instead we went out to the lake and enjoyed a relaxing evening with just each other. Later, we both commented on how it was our favorite New Years of all time.

Life is about balance.

It is about recognizing the unique being that God created you to be. It is about understanding the pieces of the puzzle that God has already laid down in front of you and respecting them. It's about having patience with the process of a new role that God may be calling you to walk in.

I should not have expected that overnight I would be able to morph from a woman who typically only took care of herself (and her cat) to a full on homemaking wife. Who did I think I was, Martha Stewart? I really messed up attempting to do everything under the sun at full speed, while forgetting that I was naïve to this whole new way of life.

Now we have a much better balance in our household. I still cook awesome homemade meals and clean, but not to such an extreme standard. I am no longer responsible for breakfast every morning, because I properly communicated to Jake that was when I needed to be able to have my God time. And he instantly understood and agreed that my quality daily God time was much more important than his omelette and pancakes.

Now when I wake up, I pour myself a cup of coffee and settle down with my Bible. It has utterly altered the trajectory of my day and as Jake likes to point out, makes me a much better wife than I was when I was tunnel-vision focused on only serving.

Some mornings I still whip up a delicious breakfast, but I do it out of love, not out of obligation. And Jake has grown to appreciate those morning meals more instead of just expecting them. We are both very knowledgeable that we still love and will go to many family and friend gatherings, but that we won't schedule them back to back to back again. No more two-a-days if we can manage and always making room during busy seasons to carve out our God time and cherish it.

The whole point that I am trying to make here is that life isn't one size fits all. What is healthy for one person to thrive could be absolutely devastating for another. It's all about trial and error. It's all about compromise, while also never compromising the most important things in your life.

God should never come second fiddle, and coming from someone who made that mistake even in the midst of good intentions, you will regret it. God is the source of life that is meant to shine brilliantly through you.

You won't be able to tap into the potential that God has for you if you are constantly trying to fit the mold of someone else. I thought that all wives had to be a certain way, but that's just not true. Every relationship is different and every definition of wife is in turn different too. Yes, the Bible still gives us great guidelines, but the details to each couple can vary.

I thought that all successful women needed to look the same, but in reality, success is defined in the eyes of the beholder. And I don't know about ya'll, but I want my beholder to be God!

God has shown me that I can be successful without having to achieve all of the worldly merits that go along with it. And lastly, the definition of "Good Christian" looks different for each of God's children. Yes, we should all spend daily time in God's word, but some people learn better from listening and others learn better from reading. And then there are also those visual learners. We should tweak our God relationship to best fit how God created us to be.

Be patient with the process, God is working a miracle through you. He is constantly working to evolve your character and teach you valuable lessons along the way.

The Grace Of God

Refraining from something is a great explanation of what patience is.

God is the greatest example of long suffering, because He refrained from enforcing His collection of the debt from our sin. Instead of inflicting His judgment upon us, that admittedly we totally deserve, God exercised forbearance and refrained by instead sending His one and only Son to die for our sins.

Many humans have a very hard time with patience, myself included. It is so much easier to feel justified and deserving, wanting to exercise your right to claim what is yours. But this immature mindset is opposed to Jesus's teachings.

This is not the way of the Spirit.

God commands us to forbear, to endure uncomfortably, and patiently wait. What are we waiting for, you might ask? Well, we are all waiting for something different, as each of us has our own struggles. I am waiting for optimal health. My childhood friend is waiting for her husband. My sister is waiting for her purpose to be revealed. My neighbor is waiting for fertility.

We each have something that we deeply long for. God wants to mature us and practice our patience with these very desires.

Patience is the reason that God chose to redeem us, instead of harshly judging us like those in the Old Testament. You and I, who should honestly be harshly judged, have no right to place judgment on others. We must work on extending this grace to the world, just like God has been merciful and grace-filled toward us.

Every single day we should ask God to help grow our patience, because I know at least once daily I am personally tested on my endurance during times of trial. God is trying to grow my stamina to stay calm during moments of adversity.

For me at least, patience is the one area that I have the hardest time exercising. In moments where your patience is tested, I challenge you to take a deep breath and pray to the Lord to help you handle whatever the situation (whether big or small) with grace. The simple act of expanding your lungs with oxygen and bringing your troubles to the Lord during your moment of frustration will truly do wonders for your ability to remain calm and Christ-like.

Always remember, an impatient person is not a very fun person to be around. Pray to the Lord to help you from losing your cool and to be able to stay calm and collected during times of trial.

Allow God to take the broken
pieces of your life and make you
whole. Grant Him permission
to create something unique and
brilliant with you.

Kindness is a lesson that we have been taught our entire lives. One of the very first lessons we learn in Kindergarten is the golden rule, "Treat others the way you want to be treated."

But does that mean that we have allowed this carnal rule to soak into the very fabric of our hearts?

Now, more than ever, we need to be kind to one another. With such sadness, I see a world torn into a million pieces. I see families broken apart and friendships forever burned. We live in a world where your opinion is your "bible". Where if someone does not act, think, or dare I say it, vote like you, then they may as well be dead to you.

This is a tragedy.

Kindness is being nice to anyone no matter the difference in culture, politics, and so forth. Everyone deserves to be looked after and shown compassion. When you cultivate a kind heart, you enable a serving spirit to preside, always showing benevolence not animosity towards others.

Jesus did not spend His life alongside perfect churchgoers, Jesus walked with the sinners. The prostitutes, tax collectors, and even murderers! Jesus loved all, even if they ridiculed Him. Even when they refused to believe who He was and what He stood for.

We need to all learn some lessons from this prime example that Jesus set for us. We are to be kind always. We are spreaders of the truth and are commanded to go into the darkness and be the light. It would be so much easier to only be around others who believe, think, and act like you. Life would be peachy. But we would be utterly missing our purpose if we only swam where the water was calm. We need to trek out into the storm. We need to sail to uncharted territories. We need to be unafraid, filled with the word, spreading love and kindness with everyone that we interact with.

I do not have the power to save someone. But Jesus does have the power to work through me, and lead someone towards their eternal salvation. If I am unkind, hateful, or judgmental then I will be robbing the Holy Spirit an opportunity to use me as a holy vessel.

In a world full of hate, show the love. In a land filled with judgment, spread kindness. Smile, even when you don't feel like it. Preach, even when uncomfortable. Serve, even when you would rather be anywhere else.

We were called to work for the Lord, not for our own selfish interests. We should be kind in our work, no matter what that be. We must be a representation of Christ, no matter where we are or what we are doing. We never know who is around to be impacted by our demeanor. God is always watching out for His Beloved Children.

Have you ever heard an unkind person start preaching the gospel? Yeah, feels pretty fake to me too.

Hypocrisy exists all around, not just within the church. However, unbelievers are very astute to pointing out when a Christian is acting in a hypocritical manner. One of the most common examples of this, is when a believer of God is acting in an unkind manner toward others. It does not matter whether they are Jesus lovers or not, we are called to always be kind.

I feel like we are beginning to define ourselves from our differences in thought. If a person does not believe or process things exactly like you, then they are faulty. This is such a sad way of acting and going on with life. We are called to be kind to one another, despite our differences.

Kindness is like a never-emptying buffet table and the world at large is starving for some genuine kindness. In such an uncouth time as these, we need more compassion to feed on. We are called to feed the hungry hearts of unbelievers with the Fruit of the Spirit. By exhibiting kindness to all those around us, we are able to glorify God without even having to speak His mighty name.

If someone hurts you, don't hurt them back. Show them the kindness that they should have also bestowed upon you. If someone makes you angry, don't lash out on them but be friendly in every interaction.

> *"But I tell you, do not resist an evil person. If anyone slaps you on the right cheek, turn to them the other cheek also." (Matthew 5:39 NIV)*

Jesus has empowered us to do our Father's work with a kind mindset. Not grumpily spewing His teachings, but altruistically enacting them through every move that we make.

The more you begin to act in kind ways (even when you don't want to) the more you will begin to truly have a kind heart. Kindness will seep out of you, even in the smallest of interactions.

My husband is a great representation of this. I, like most people, despise spam calls. When people from call centers try to trick you and trap you into a conversation or purchase, it just grinds my bones because in the past I would naively fall for it every time.

Now I find myself getting so annoyed, and I either do not answer the phone or quickly hang up within the first few seconds after I say, "Hello?" This is not very kind of me, and I really need to work on it.

However, my husband, being both the patient and nice human being that he is, acts in a completely opposite manner. When he answers a scam call, he not only is polite.

Oh no, he goes above and beyond that.

He also asks them how their day is, and although declining the service they are prodding to provide, he has a kind interaction with each of them. Sometimes he even asks if there is something that he can pray with them about!

Jake does not like these calls any more than I do, but he always acts in a kind and respectful manner towards disengaging these unwanted conversations. I really respect that about him, and have been trying to emulate that sense of both patience and gentleness in conversations that I would rather not be having.

Kindness Is A Holy Weapon

When it is my time to go and meet Jesus, there should be no sadness. Thinking about it now, my human self will mourn the life that I will be ending with the people I love dearly. But I also know that this human life we are all living is full of pain and heartache. The trials and tribulations that we all encounter are difficult to weather at times.

I know that whenever God calls me home, I will go gratefully. I will sprint full speed (which is a big deal because I despise running) into the welcoming arms of Jesus. I will weep tears of utter joy and gratitude as Jesus holds me in His soothing embrace.

There is no need to be sad when a loved one goes on to live with the Lord in their forever home. By accepting Jesus as your Lord and Savior, you are granted a never-expiring ticket to everlasting life.

You see, we may all be mortal now. Slowly dying each and every day, whether or not we are sick. But one day our bodies riddled with illness, the passing of time, and sin will be made brand new.

We will be made whole again.

Kind of like when you are baptized and your soul is made brand new. You are born again spiritually.

"…Though your sins are like scarlet, they will be as white as snow;
though they are red as crimson, they will be like wool."
(Isaiah 1:18 HCSB)

When I was baptized and rededicated my life to following Christ, I had an awe-inspiring experience in the holy water. When the pastor dipped me back into the water, behind my closed eyelids I experienced the brightest light that I couldn't even begin to describe. It was white, but not. Bright and brilliant, but not overwhelming. Glowing and warm, yet also energizing and electrifying.

In the brief span of time that I was under the water with my eyes closed, dedicating myself to my precious Lord, I know that I was given a glimpse of the brilliance of God. I was given a teaser of Heaven, of the splendor that is waiting for the Lord's children just on the other side.

Although on Earth your soul is renewed through baptism, your body is not made brand new until you are reunited with your Creator in Heaven. And by golly, do I look forward to the day I get to fall to my knees at my Father's feet.

The moment that I was designed for.

But I also immensely value my fragile life, the one that I am trying to live out to the fullest right now. As long as God graces me with breath in my lungs, I will sing His praise. I know I was put here to do many good works for the Kingdom, and gee-whiz, I am only just getting started! I dedicated my life to the Lord, enlisting as a soldier in His glorious army. I am ready to fight for the faith and to never stop working for my gracious God.

There were so many years where I wasted time. I lived with an utterly selfish mindset, only trying to think about what I could get out of this life, instead of what I could give through my life.

I wish I had come to some of these life-altering realizations sooner. Because every day that I get to wake up loving on my family, the Lord, and God's Kingdom, is the best day ever.

Don't be like me.

Please don't make the same fatal mistakes that I repeated for decades. Be selfless. Be kind. Be trusting. Be strong. Give your heart, love, and everything you do to God. Allow Him to take the broken pieces of your life and make you whole. Grant Him permission to create something unique and brilliant with you.

Stop trying to cram your feet into shoes that weren't designed to fit you! Stop striving to be who you think you should be and just simply allow God to mold you into who He wants you to become.

Our time on Earth is so fleeting.

> *"Why, you do not even know what will happen tomorrow. What is your life? You are a mist that appears for a little while and then vanishes."* (James 4:14 NIV)

Don't waste your mist! Don't allow your legacy to be only about status, reputation, net worth, materialism, and pride. Don't feed into the evil of the world by only living up to ridiculous worldly standards.

We inhabit a broken society, and the sooner you come to realize that fact, the sooner you will want to be part of the change. You will want to make a difference for the Kingdom of God. You will want to help to lead lost souls to the loving redemption of Jesus Christ.

The real rulers of the world are unable to be seen. At least not right now. But they are the ones of true power. They are the ones you should be serving. Control is a sham. Trust me, you don't want absolute control over your life. Yes, God loves you so much that He has given us the gift of free will, but give it back! Ask for a refund. It's scary and many times downright awful when we determine that we are the sole ones in control of our lives and destiny.

It's too much pressure for me!

God's plan is infinitely a million times greater than even the best plan that you could come up with for yourself.

Real self-control is knowing when to relinquish control. The true measure of your own power is coming to the sobering realization that you really don't have as much power as you would have previously liked to have thought.

Don't you want to be on the winning side of the biggest battle of the world? I know I sure as heck do!

Let me give you a little visualization that has helped me to comprehend this epic spiritual battle that is raging right here, right now, between good and evil.

When I think of this spiritual battle my mind instantly thinks of a calm sea. Of midnight blue ocean water stretching out in all directions as far as the eye can see. The water is calm and glass-like all around, with not a boat, bird, or person in sight. The water looks so peaceful and inviting from the surface, mesmerizing and tantalizing.

Just by looking at the serene body of water, you can feel a rush of peace wash over you. Gently soothing your soul. This is what Jesus does for us. This is the very reason He died on the cross for our sins. He wanted us to be above the cold deep ocean water. He did not want us to have to endure what all lurked below the surface.

Unknown to the naked eye, this picturesque ocean is filled with terrible nasty creatures. Monstrosities that will bite you, shredding you apart limb from limb with their innumerable rows of razor sharp teeth. If you were to be allowed to dive into that water, you would be drug down, to depths you didn't even know possible to exist.

We all know that the ocean is filled with more creatures than we can even count. Heck, the majority of the ocean on Earth has yet to even be explored! There are hundreds of thousands of species that we can't begin to fathom, completely beyond comprehension of even our wildest imaginations. Yet they still exist. They are still there, whether we see them or not. We even recognize that there is much we do not know and most likely will never fully discover about the mysterious waters that cover the Earth.

The ocean is filled with daily battles for survival among species. Some marine animals kill for food while others just simply kill for fun. A war is waging underneath the ocean, yet all we see on the surface is a calm flat expanse of serenity.

This is what the spiritual battle that is going on is like. We humans are above the ocean; we only see the mere surface to an infinitely deep battlefield. The battles being waged in the spiritual realm are very real, much like the creatures of the deep blue. It's happening, whether we are going to humble ourselves and be smart enough to admit it or not.

God is fighting for you in the spiritual realm. He has an army of angels who are swimming below the surface, savagely engaging in the war for your soul.

Many people are scared of the ocean, and rightly so. My two irrational fears are midnight black dark water and sharks. Thus, being trapped in the middle of the ocean at night, treading water in a shark infested area would be the definition of my worst nightmare.

But do I let these fears stop me from diving into the refreshing ocean waters any chance that I get? No, absolutely not! Will I still surf, snorkel, jet ski, tube, and even swim with stingrays in the middle of the ocean with no land in sight? Yup, you betcha!

I know that sharks exist, and unfortunately for my blood pressure I have swum in the general close vicinity of them at least two times (that I know of!), but that doesn't stop me from going in the ocean.

With that in mind, I know that the biggest spiritual battle is raging on, but that doesn't stop me from doing God's work. Just because spirits and demons and the devil himself hate me and are doing everything in their power for me to fail, does not mean I give up and cower in the corner. No, if anything that means that I need to stand taller and armor up.

I *will* be of assistance to God and His army in this war!

The creatures of the deep blue are there, hunting and preying on the weak, whether you want to acknowledge it or not. Sorry, these are just the facts. Just because you decide to never dip your toes in the ocean, does not mean that others aren't suffering. So what if instead of just simply looking out at the clear "calm" waters, you hopped on a boat, grabbed a spear and some nets, and helped to kill those beasts even from the ocean's surface?

Then not only would good be fighting under the surface (God's angel army in the spirit realm) but we as believers of Christ would be able to battle in the physical realm also.

As my husband, the sports aficionado loves to say, "Let's move from the defense to the offense." We need to stop waiting for an attack in order to make a counter protective move. Not good enough, we need to don God's armor, grab some sharp spears, and join in, enlisting our service for the good fight.

> *"Put on the full armor of God, so that you can take your stand against the devil's schemes." (Ephesians 6:11 NIV*

Be Kind To The Child Within

Kindness does not only have to do with others. Yes, we should always be kind to those around us. But it is just as important to learn to also be kind to yourself.

Humans are erroneous in nature. We unconsciously make a list of all of our shortcomings and faults and hold ourselves to our own personal fire of self-disappointment.

In order to practice being kind to yourself, you must change the way you talk to yourself. Many times, we are our own worst enemy. I cannot count the number of times I have heard a friend say they are stupid, fat, untalented, unimpressive... I mean for real, the depressing list goes on and on!

It makes my skin crawl when I encounter other people spewing such garbage onto their own lives and demeaning their character.

However, this is totally the pot calling the kettle black, because I used to do it too! I too am guilty of saying awful about myself, unknowingly giving others permission to speak that way about me also.

Ladies, we have to stop being mean to ourselves!

Being kind to ourselves and others goes hand-in-hand. Jesus was not loving to all of the sinners and then hateful to himself, that would be going against all of His teachings! We can't love on everyone around us and kindly encourage their growth while also treating ourselves horribly behind closed doors.

It just doesn't work that way!

What you say to your friends, the positive "pump up" conversations you give them, should be the exact same self-talk that you give yourself.

An idle mind is the devil's playground. Are your thoughts creating momentum in your life or holding you back? Change the way you talk to yourself. Compliment yourself.

Think about it this way, "Would you say that to a child?"

I used to think I was very weak, both mentally, physically, and spiritually. I used to always count myself out or bully myself because of how lacking I perceived my self-worth to be, which was an absolute lie that the enemy was ensnaring me to believe. God has now shown me just how spectacular and mighty He created me to be.

Now when I am feeling a moment of self-doubt or insecurity, I chant to myself, "You are strong. You are brave. You are courageous."

Just by giving myself these reaffirming beliefs, that I know to be true even if I am not feeling it in that specific moment, does absolute wonders for me. Instead of feeding the festering trap the enemy was trying to cage me in, I am able to build myself up and help to mentally free myself from his clutches.

Self-love is so important because true self-love comes from God.

Jesus wants us to be kind to others and kind to ourselves. The only way to truly embody this aspect of the Fruit of the Spirit is to perform both of these aspects simultaneously.

Our God is a lavishly loving God who delights in doing kind things for us. Not because He has to, but because He wants to. Because he loves us and takes pleasure in fulfilling our dreams and putting a smile on His beloved children's faces.

God is kind, not because he is looking for something in return, but because He wants to bless us. God is genuinely kindhearted, and He yearns for us to be kindhearted in our actions too.

> *"But when the kindness of God our Savior and His love for mankind appeared, He saved us - not by works of righteousness that we had done, but according to His mercy - through the washing of regeneration and renewal by the Holy Spirit." (Titus 3:4-5 HCSB)*

Set out every day to make the world a little better of a place, to put a smile on the faces of those who encounter you, and to allow God's goodness to overflow through your life.

Goodness is not something you are born with; it's something you must cultivate. Like a marathon runner, training every day, racing along on grueling trails. You don't just wake up one day and decide to run 26.2 miles. Goodness is intentional - it is the conscious decision of choosing right over wrong, and having a true desire to help others.

It's the active enactment of choosing to set our hearts on the things above, as we stumble through the world below. Goodness prevailing over evil is proof of the Spirit of God residing in us.

I now know God is going to do a good and wonderful work through me.

I used to struggle with thinking that I wasn't capable of being good and bringing more goodness into this world. I was conceived through sin, my young parents both new to college and to the fresh oyster of the world just beginning to open in front of them. I was an absolute accident. Unplanned, unprepared for and possibly for even a brief millisecond, unwanted.

I grew up with the word "mistake" stamped onto my forehead.

My parents never ended up staying together, and although they tried, it just didn't end up working. For a long time, I blamed myself for that. Wondering if I was never accidentally conceived, that maybe they would have ended up together and been a real family.

I was never ashamed of my family, but I was ashamed of myself, and the problems that my existence caused. I remember with vivid clarity when we would play games during P.E. in elementary school. There was this one game where all of the children would line up on one side of the gym and the coach would call out questions for the children. If the answer to the question was yes, the student would get to step forward five steps. Whichever child reached the other side of the gym first, won. Every time we would play this game, my heart would get a little heavy.

The coach would yell out the fateful question, "Alright kids, are your parents married?"

So many kids would step forward, and in my mind I would be left in the dust.

As the years went on and divorce became more prevalent the above question would then be followed by, "Are your parents divorced?"

And while other children would move forward, I would still stay stagnant. My feet feeling stuck in quicksand, wishing I could just disappear on the spot.

My parents were neither married nor divorced. It was a hard realization for my young naïve mind to comprehend, and it left me with some scar-tissue based off of self-guilt and blame.

I don't know what it's like to have a single nuclear family, I have always had multiple.

I have never experienced a Christmas where I didn't have to leave the family that I had woken up to, to be taken to my other family in the afternoon and do it all over again. Trying to muster the same amount of enthusiasm and gusto as the first time earlier that morning.

In one family "Yes Sir" and "No Ma'am" was the requirement,

while in the other you would get a funny look for being so formal. I grew up in such a state of confusion, having to morph my personality to fit whichever side of the family I was currently with. I was resentful and rebellious towards my situation for much of my childhood, angry at the cards I had been dealt.

Throughout most of my childhood I struggled to accept and adopt the unique living and parenting situation that I was in. It was very hard for me to adjust between two completely different households. For such a long time I viewed my situation for only the bad that I experienced through it, not recognizing the good that was coming from it.

I can now comprehend that I was created for a very specific reason. That the households that I experienced growing up helped me to form a holistic overview of what different parenting methods look like. You see, both sets of parents loved me - there is no question about that - but one parenting type was love-based and the other was fear-based.

In one household voices were never raised and in the other, yelling was very common. In one house there were weekly chores and you continuously were being told how much of a privilege it was for you to have the everyday essentials that you did and the other house was serving and generous, with no strings attached or expected responsibilities other than keeping a clean room. Which let's be honest, my messy self still rarely did. In one house you got spanked with the belt and in the other a hand was never laid on you and punishment came in the form of sitting down in the office and having a discussion.

Through all of these parenting differences and opposite living environments, I constantly had to be adaptable and fluid. At first, I used to loathe having to be two different people and needing to learn the trait of being able to be a social chameleon. But now, I recognize that I developed and matured a trait that greatly has been able to serve me into adulthood.

Now, no matter the social situation I can be comfortable and network, adapt, and market with a whole slew of different characters. Also, because of being able to have a first-hand experience between two totally different parenting styles, I have a healthy understanding of what I do and absolutely don't want to do when I become a parent myself.

And although I have a huge family, and sometimes it's still overwhelming to make sure to see everyone during the holidays, I wouldn't wish for it to be any other way. You see, both of my stepparents have been in my life since I was eighteen months old. So in reality, I actually have four parents. I have never known a life without my step mother and step father. And with their presence came the added bonus of their amazing families as well, who so kindly took me in as their own, wholeheartedly treating me as kin.

I have begun to cherish and treasure the uniqueness of God's plan for my family life, because God blessed me with double the people to love and be loved by.

Even in the midst of a tough situation, God can still display His goodness. It took me a while to recognize the silver lining in my situation, but now I am grateful for the unique childhood that I had.

I am abundantly blessed with many wonderful family members. I have a plethora of different outlets of family who love and accept me. And that is truly such a wonderful feeling. I also have knowledge that most people don't get in regards to different household styles and parenting types.

I know that what at first was perceived as bad, truly turned out to be one of my biggest blessings. God wanted me to experience what all I went through in my childhood. These events helped to chisel and shape the woman of God that He created me to blossom into.

I hate to be cliché, but I turned some of the sourest lemons into the most refreshing lemonade. God wants to turn my mess into my message. I know that He needed me to grow up in the manner that I did so that I could better serve His kingdom with my testimony.

Heck, my parents conceived me at a point in their lives when it would have been much easier to just get an abortion and be done with it. They both were fresh out of high school, embarking on their new college journeys - still trying to figure out who they were and what they wanted to do with their lives. I was the last thing on their minds or in their plans.

But God wanted me to be born when I was. God wanted to use the genetic makeup of both my Mother and Father to uniquely create me. His plan did not destine them to be together, and although as a young child I used to wish it were so, I now fully appreciate the fact that they never ended up together. I wholeheartedly believe their paths only crossed so that I could be created and put on this Earth.

Although I have two siblings on my Mom's side, and two siblings on my Dad's side, neither of them have my genetic makeup. I despise using the term half-sibling because my brothers and sisters are every bit as much mine, as I am theirs. But straight genetically speaking, I am an only child. I am the one and done. An absolute original with no remakes.

God needed me to be put on this Earth, intertwined with the families I was placed with for a very specific reason. The Lord always knows what He's doing, and it took me a long time to appreciate that fact.

> *"And in view of this, we always pray for you that our God will consider you worthy of His calling, and will, by His power, fulfill every desire for goodness and work of faith, so that the name of our Lord Jesus will be glorified by you, and you by Him, according to the grace of our God and the Lord Jesus Christ." (2 Thessalonians 1:11 HCSB)*

I was created to serve God and fulfill the purpose that He has destined for my life from the very moment that I came out of the womb.

But let's be honest. This book isn't about me.

Yes, my testimony is imbued throughout these chapters so that you can understand me better and see how God has worked through my own testimony.

However, this book is about you and for you.

You were born very specially too. You were crafted with the very genetic makeup that you have, expertly made to have the likes, talents, and dreams that you possess. God wants you to develop the traits He has created for you to cultivate.

God wants you to start understanding the hidden goodness in your life, that has always been there even through the harder times of your existence. He wants you to find the good in yourself, in your circumstances, and in others. He wants you to not only do the right thing, but make things right by convicting others to do good in a gentle manner.

You were created to be honest, honorable, and full of integrity.

This life we all are living is filled with both good and bad. God is closer now, more than ever, but evil also lurks in the shadows. You must learn to choose the good. Must recognize the goodness that is dwelling within yourself and all around you.

This is a lesson you must commit to for your entire life.

Jesus First

The other day I was in a mood. A little hormonal, I might add. I was in the shower and just being crappy. In my head, I had so much attitude it was unreal.

I can't even remember what I was upset about, but I just know it's what Jake and I would label a "Code Red Moment".

I was upset at Jake over something, probably very silly. And I was venting in the shower to Jesus, asking him sassily to help me to show my husband the love that I should show him, instead of treating him with the current contempt that I was experiencing in the moment.

Jesus frankly spoke to me, "How can you be intimate with your husband if you are not intimate with me first? You will never understand how to properly love him until you love me more."

Whewey, did I instantly feel a hot strike of conviction in my feisty self!

In premarital counseling, we were always taught that the love that we have for one another is from God. Like a triangle, we have to go to God in order to then get to our spouse. That is the way that love, marriage, and intimacy is supposed to be structured.

The Holy hierarchy, so to speak.

In order for the love in my marriage and for my husband to grow stronger, I had to learn to love Jesus more. I needed to strengthen my intimacy with Jesus, and then I would be able to be a better spouse, with more love and ultimately grace to give to my husband.

I'll be the first to admit that I'm nowhere near perfect. I'm still maturing and growing spiritually, and I do sometimes have an attitude that my poor husband tries his best to deflect. We are both human, and sometimes we don't always handle situations the best.

But what I am beginning to truly understand, is that if I do not put Jesus before my husband, then I am ultimately doing Jake a disservice.

My Gram once told me that I need never settle for a man. That I will know who my husband was intended to be because he will make it clear that he will never love me as much as he loves God.

I remember the very moment that she said this to me, in the comfort of her cozy living room, with the smell of savory essential oils wafting through the air.

I also distinctly remember internally rolling my eyes as she said this. Thinking, "Yeah okayyyy, like there is even a man out there like that?! Maybe older men can get to that point but all of the men I have encountered have never had a heart after God in that manner."

But I just nodded and agreed, deep down hoping that she was right. That one day I could locate my husband, a man created to love God more than me.

I can vividly remember the exact moment now. Jake and I together, holding hands tightly and gazing adoringly into each other's big brown eyes. Suddenly, he admitted that he had to tell me something. Immediately my hands began to sweat, nervous for whatever bomb of information he was about to drop on me.

I turned away, afraid to meet his eyes as he said, "I just want you to know that I love you and I always will. But I need you to understand that you will never be the first love in my life."

My heart dropped, instantly I felt my face flush, and tears well up into my eyes. When he noticed my quivering lip, he quickly added, "I will always put God first, no matter what. That doesn't mean that I won't love you, but I need you to be okay that you won't be first and that will never change. My relationship and love for God will forever stay on top and I felt like I should communicate that with you."

A waterfall of large hot black tears gushed down my face, taking my mascara along with it. Now it was Jake's turn to be frazzled, his thick eyebrows knit together in concern and I could hear him audibly gulp.

But my tears were no longer tears from sadness or fear. No - these tears were produced from sheer disbelief and gratitude. Instantly my Gram's words flashed through my mind, and the "ding ding ding we have a winner!" roared loudly through my head.

I had already known Jake was to be my husband. Quite honestly, the Holy Spirit revealed it to me the very night we met. But this specific moment was the confirmation that I had been waiting for. The moment that solidified in stone, everything that I had already been suspecting. Jake Panko, my sweet love dove, was indeed created specifically to love me. But even better, he was created to put God first and cherish Him more than he would ever cherish me.

And that right there, was the best gift I could ever receive.

God is so good. He is so faithful in the promises that He fulfills in our lives. God knew that I would not feel absolutely right about who I was to marry if these exact words were not spoken to me. God knew that I sought for a man that was after His Heavenly Father's heart, before my own.

And although I had previously understood that it was important to make sure that my spouse put God first, I think sometimes I slip up myself. Like I have mentioned multiple times throughout this book, God never stops working on you. If there is a point where you feel like you are done growing, then I hate to break it to ya sister, but you have just hit a rut.

We should never stop growing!

The pressures of marriage, learning how to be a wife, and just adapting to this new way of living has been a little challenging. Sometimes I have found that in the pursuit of making my husband the happiest he can be, I might be unintentionally putting him above God. And I never want to do that!

So when Jesus gently, yet firmly, reminded me that in order to have the best marriage possible, and be the best wife, I needed to honor my love to Him first before Jake. I knew I had slipped up again, as this very simple point is sometimes easy to overlook.

Although my intentions here were good, they had gotten all backwards. Remember, God first. Husband second.

Our Lord is so good to us. And when we go to Him with our problems, instead of venting to the world, He will give us applicable solutions to better our lives and walk with Him. I have found that the days when I am spiritually filled, I am a much less contentious person.

When I begin my day with the goodness of God's word, then I am in essence filling up my spiritual cup. When my cup is full, I will have an abundance of goodness to pour out onto others' lives.

I used to try and pour from an empty cup, and that would leave me drained and cranky. By beginning the day with putting the Lord first, not my husband, not social media, not my to-do list, and not even my love for eating a hearty breakfast. But by making the conscious decision to give God my full attention in the morning, I find that the day runs much smoother.

Yes, there will still be bumps in the road of your daily lives, but by purposefully filling up your spiritual cup, you will find that the annoying things of life are a lot easier to handle. Running late because you are stuck in traffic will no longer feel like the end of the world, as it's a great time to have a worship concert in your car or call your Grandma and give her a little extra love. Spilling your coffee on your new blouse, although still annoying and scalding hot, will allow you to laugh at your silliness, as it's only clothes.

My Dad has always said this one phrase to me all growing up when I would get frazzled, "Remember, life is good."

Your life is good. You are good. God would not create you, His precious child, to be any other way. There is goodness in your soul that is just waiting to be spilled over into the world.

I truly believe the more good you put into the world, the more good you will get out of it.

Instead of sneering at the homeless on your way to an appointment, why not smile at them? Or better yet, roll down the window and ask for their name and say you will be praying for them.

Jake and I have Angel Bags that we keep in the back of our cars, that are filled with essentials like food, water, and toiletries. They also include a little salvation prayer and devotional. The individuals that we have given these to, have surprised us immensely with the tears of joy just from being thought of. By bringing goodness into their lives, which were pretty dark and lost, we are able to shine Jesus' light on them. We are able to help fill up their spiritual cup.

If you aren't comfortable with the homeless thing, I do understand. I felt that way too as a young woman going to serve under the Bridge back when I lived in Austin, Texas.

Goodness can come in the form of purchasing the person's meal behind you and telling the cashier to tell them that, "God loves them and to have a blessed day." Goodness is offering to help load the groceries of an old woman into her car and return her cart for her. Goodness is even just asking your server at your favorite Italian food restaurant if there is anything that you can pray for her about.

Just by being compassionate and loving, kind and good, you will be able to touch a lot of hearts. And I promise, yours will be moved too. The more good I bring into the world, the closer I get to understanding the goodness of Jesus and His unconditional love for us.

In a lost world, there is still goodness everywhere. We just have to know where to look for it.

"In the same way, let your light shine before men, so that they may see your good works and give glory to your Father in heaven."
(Matthew 5:16 HCSB)

Next time you make awkward eye contact with a stranger, smile. Next time you're getting a latte at Starbucks, also pay for the order behind you and leave a nice message for them to receive. Next time you feel tempted to be in a bad mood, text 3 of your friends or family and say something that you admire about them.

In a world filled with bad, be contagious in your overflowing goodness. Let the goodness of God shine through you like a bright light, battling the darkness of corruption and selfishness. God's goodness promises hope and resurrection.

It's like that saying, "God is good all the time. And all the time, God is good."

You, my sweet friend, are very good too. You have so much light and love to contribute to the world.

Set out every day to make the world a little better of a place, to put a smile on the faces of those who encounter you, and to allow God's goodness to overflow through your life.

Give God your whole heart, and you won't even be able to imagine what he will do with it! Have faith always, let your faith overflow into every circumstance and instance in your life.

A re you a faithful person?

If someone was describing you, would they say that you are dependable, devoted, and consistent? That if they found themselves in a pickle, you could be counted on to help them?

You see, our God is a very faithful God. He is always there for us, no matter what. He does not cherry-pick who He helps or who He listens to.

> *"God is faithful; you were called by Him into fellowship with His Son, Jesus Christ our Lord." (1 Corinthians 1:9 HCSB)*

Being a faithful person means setting your judgments and opinions aside and being reliable in both your relationship with God and with others. Sadly, I feel that nowadays many people struggle with justifying the help that they are willing to give.

"Does that homeless person deserve this $20 bill or will they just use it on drugs and alcohol?"

I am guilty of the above thought, which is just one example of a way that I am inadvertently putting myself above another person. Being the judge of whether they are worthy of my charity.

This is so wrong! I am not superior to anyone!

If I give a $20 bill from the goodness of my heart, then it doesn't matter what is done with it. Yes, I would prefer for it to go towards giving a person in need some quality nutrition and care, but once it's out of my hands I cannot allocate where it goes. It is just simply about giving with a generous heart and content mind. And what I have found, if you don't feel persuaded to give cash then an angel bag or a hot meal will also go a very long way for someone in need that you may be internally struggling with being generous towards.

When someone is in need, we should prove to be faithful of character and give. We should help those who need help. This doesn't mean help everyone with just anything. As the Bible says that we are to handle our own daily burdens, but if someone is truly struggling, then we are to go and help them with what is unbearable for them.

> *"Dear brothers and sisters, if another believer is overcome by some sin, you who are godly should gently and humbly help that person back on the right path. And be careful not to fall into the same temptation yourself. Share each other's burdens, and in this way obey the law of Christ. If you think you are too important to help someone, you are only fooling yourself. You are not that important. Pay careful attention to your own work, for then you will get the satisfaction of a job well done, and you won't need to compare yourself to anyone else. For we are each responsible for our own conduct." (Galatians 6:1-4 NLT)*

It took me a long time to understand and differentiate what was being said in this Bible verse. But through a book that has really been helping me to grow stronger in who God created me to be, *Boundaries* by Dr. John Townsend and Dr. Henry Cloud, I have been able to figure out the difference.

We must learn to be faithful to lending a helping hand to those who are truly in need of the services we can offer. No, you don't need me to clean your house just because you are overwhelmed and don't want to make the time to do it. But yes, if you are struggling through chemo, and having a very hard time moving throughout your day, I will gladly show up on your doorstep, cleaning products in hand (natural cleaning products, ladies, chemicals are bad for you!) and start scrubbing.

How can the Fruit of the Spirit develop and grow in our lives if we are not faithful in its fruition? The Fruit may never ripen if our faith is wavering.

We live in a world where seeing is associated with believing. Where in order to have trust and faith in something, we must have tangible proof. But this is not faith at all! Faith is the hope and trust in things unseen. It is the very opposite of what is ingrained into our minds from today's society and standards of living.

Jesus is the best example of allowing the Spirit to flourish and produce Fruit in His life. Through His unwavering trust and obedience, He provided the ultimate expression of faithfulness through the Holy Spirit, when He offered Himself on the cross, dying for our sins and providing each one of us with the opportunity for eternal life in Heaven.

God has called us, no—scratch that— commanded us, to exhibit our faith in the very same way. We are provided with the very same Spirit that Jesus was anointed with, so that we too can be empowered to stand justly for God's causes. We must be steadfast in our certainty of the truth, maturing in our walk with Jesus. We must rise above the lowly standards of the world, and hold ourselves to a Heavenly status.

Yes, I hate to break it to you, but we will all end up falling short. We are human, we'll make mistakes and still sin. But we must hold this truth dear to our hearts, because nothing we will ever do will make God unfaithful towards us. He will always have our back, and now it's time that we armor up and fight for His truth to be freely shared throughout this broken world.

The Fruit planted in our hearts is steadfast, a loyal covenant with God Himself. We are immeasurably lucky that God's Fruit is growing within us. We must continue to strengthen our faith, so that His Fruit can feed not only ourselves but also the multitude of starving souls around us. Our fidelity in the Lord will help us to share His faithfulness with the entire world.

"Because of the Lord's faithful love, we do not perish, for His mercies never end. They are new every morning; great is Your faithfulness." (Lamentations 3:22-23 HCSB)

I believe, no - forget that - I KNOW that God puts certain desires into our hearts so that when He fulfills them we can glorify His name with our testimony. I have been so blessed these past few years, as the Lord has taught me this generous lesson more times than I can count.

As mentioned in a previous chapter, I truly feel that faith and patience go hand-in-hand. In order to truly be patient, you must strengthen your faith.

My Wedding Days

My husband and I are somewhat of a unique couple. We had multiple weddings. Not because we needed to, but because we were blessed enough to be able to have our comprehensive wedding dreams come true.

You see, Jake and I both have the most spectacular moments with God when we are alone together, lost in the beauty of God's nature. So for our wedding we really wanted to make it all about the most important things, our love for the Lord and one another.

I have a large family and although wonderful, being with them all together was an anxiety-producing imagination. I am most comfortable in a smaller group of people, and I wanted my focus for the day to be all about honoring the love that God blessed us with in each other. I wanted to respect the covenant we were making, with no distractions.

The creation of the Holy Trinity that Jake and I were entering into was of utmost importance to us, and we wanted our sole focus to be on that fact alone. Not focusing on trying not to trip while walking down the aisle with everyone's eyes on me or making sure to try and thank every guest who came.

The little girl inside of me of course wanted that big wedding spectacle, but I also desired to honor God first and foremost with my marriage. So Jake and I decided to elope. Although I don't know if it can really be considered eloping, since we did tell all the parents about it beforehand.

Alas, just the two of us, and my wedding dress shoved into the overhead bin of the plane, jetted off to the romantic rolling hills of Italy. We said our vows to one another in a jasmine, vine covered gazebo overlooking the sparkling water of Lake Como.

It was the best moment of my entire life.

That whole day felt truly like Heaven on Earth. We had our special union captured by a videographer, just so that we could make sure to always remember the day all of our dreams came true. I have watched that video probably over 300 times, and I tear up during every single viewing because it's the moment I truly took my first flight as a butterfly.

You can see our video on my website **www.thehappyhotmess.com** if interested. I watch it at least once a week, to remind myself that it was indeed real. That dreams really do come true, and happily ever after's do exist.

Yes, those fairytales are still hard work and filled with learning moments. But true love is real, Jesus is the first to display it to us and if we truly accept Him into our hearts then He will teach us how to give that same kind of love to others.

I never knew how to love, until I knew Jesus.

I was 100% myself that day. I did my own hair and makeup. I walked down to the song *Here Comes The Sun,* which Jake was expertly playing off of his iPhone. We laughed through our handwritten wedding vows, just being our goofy selves the entire time, not worried about what we looked like or how we acted. We both had difficulty getting our rings on, as Jake put mine on very obviously backwards and I couldn't get his over the bump in this knuckle from when he had previously hurt his finger in a football game and gotten surgery on it. We both giggled like little schoolgirls at our funny mishaps, and by the end of that glorious day our cheeks hurt from smiling.

All around, it was a dream come true, and we think of that blessed day very often, as we felt God's presence from the moment we woke up that morning and did a Bible study, while drinking Italian espressos, to the evening with the chilly lake breeze gently kissing our cheeks as we had a candlelit dinner underneath the brilliant stars.

On both of our wedding days, God blessed me with a beautiful crescendo to my butterfly message.

On our more traditional wedding day, a month later in Texas, surrounded by all of our friends and family, the refreshing November air was blowing the softest breeze throughout the audience. As my husband pointed out during our vows, the sun was sparkling radiantly on me while I was standing at the altar. Almost like God himself was shining down a spotlight for the bride alone.

And as I began to read my handwritten vows, the most miraculous thing happened.

Hundreds - I'm not kidding - *hundreds* of butterflies began to fly right behind the altar. They seemed to come from almost every direction, and they were stunning. They were so graceful and peaceful. The Holy Spirit was alive and tangible throughout our entire service, the presence of our Lord very apparent to not only us, but the entire audience.

After our beautiful ceremony concluded and we began the task of taking a thousand family portraits, someone even came up to my Dad as the guests were proceeding into the reception area and asked how much it cost for the awesome butterfly release. Many people thought we had paid to make that miracle happen!

I have come to recognize with a humble and grateful heart, that our God is a most romantic Father. If you give Him your heart and trust in His plan for your life, you will be pleasantly surprised. Our Lord is so faithful, intimate, and intricate in His splendid plans.

He alone has made every romantic moment of our lives, a million times more wonderful.

Man, I wish I had room to list all of the instances where God has sprinkled some brilliant fairy-tale pizzazz onto our lives. One day I will detail all of these events in a book regarding the full Panko love story, and how we came to be husband and wife. But for now, please take my word on it.

Give God your whole heart, and you won't even be able to imagine what he will do with it!

Thank you Lord for being so faithful to me. Thank you for blessing me with things I do not deserve. Thank you for showing me love that I only thought existed in make believe.

Ladies, if God did it for me, then he sure as heck can (and WILL) do it for you too. Just have faith always, let your faith overflow into every circumstance and instance in your life.

God will surprise you.

Gentleness is actually a quiet strength, an ability to keep your composure during times of adversity.

G entleness is a very misunderstood term in the Christian faith. There are many misconceptions around the true meaning of this word, and the best ways with which to put it into application in our everyday lives.

Gentleness is many times thought to be interchangeable with weakness. These words are quite opposite believe it or not. Gentleness is actually a quiet strength, an ability to keep your composure during times of adversity.

Many be of the opinion that in order to exercise gentleness within the parameters of Christian faith, they must become a doormat. That in the face of confrontation they must roll over, unable to engage in combat.

What a bunch of crap!

You must understand this, when we become Christians, we enlist into God's army. Right now, at this very second, the most savage and relentless spiritual battle of all time is taking place. Forces of evil are fighting for the unknowing souls of mankind. This battle is brutal and you best believe that it's not being fought gently. Swords are being wielded with strength and a vicious determination that many of us do not even have the ability to comprehend.

Being gentle does not mean being less than. It means containing the strength of the Spirit in a masterful way. It means overcoming your battles not with harsh empty threats but with sharpened weapons created to destroy the enemy. It is capable of fighting battles, standing strong in your faith, and being gentle while doing it.

Gentleness is a direct measure of how much of God's identity is able to shine through you. You are allowed to fight a battle, but do it from a place of tranquility within the Spirit. You are able to voice your opinion, but do it from a graceful and serene heart.

Being gentle in demeanor is actually a quiet strength that many fail to recognize and harness. I have found that being gentle is the best way to connect with others and grow deeper relationships.

If you grew up in a house full of athletes like I did, then you also learned a lot about tough love and constructive criticism. Some people respond very well to this, and others don't. I am in the latter category. If I am working hard for a sport or doing a workout and I get yelled at to work harder, run faster, or do more reps because I am not applying myself then I instinctively want to stop. I will stubbornly walk off the field, quickly turn off that treadmill, or drop those weights. When I get yelled at, even in a sports-like setting I just freeze.

My brain goes, "Nope. I'm done."

I surprisingly have quite a bit of athletic ability, but I just cease to use it in team settings because I do not perform well with the tough-love mindset that is so common throughout the sports world.

If you were to encourage and lift me up, I would gladly score that goal, push myself to run farther than I ever have before, or do more reps than you even thought possible. However, in our culture many believe that being tough, raising your voice, and using intimidation as a factor for success, is more effective than being gentle, kind, and uplifting.

Just like in sports, I believe this is the same in relationships. Growing up, I experienced quite a bit of tough love. The "suck it up, it's not as bad as you think" mentality. This way of parenting really made me feel invalidated in my feelings. That the pains that I was experiencing weren't worthy of being heard. In turn, making me feel like I wasn't worthy. And thus, I began to altogether hide parts of my life (parts that I should have been sharing) with my parents.

When someone is struggling or hurting, they don't need tough love. They don't want to hear a calloused response such as, "Oh stop crying. It's not the end of the world." They want you to hug them and possibly even cry with them. They want you to be empathetic and gentle with them by acting in a tender manner towards their hurting heart and wounded feelings.

Gentleness is the best way to build trust. It is such an important tool to use when trying to grow closer to someone. People don't want to open up to harsh personalities who will belittle and judge their struggles. No, they will feel more comfortable letting their guard down with a gentle spirit. Gentleness is the key to having meaningful, honest, and open conversations in your life.

"Be happy with those who are happy, and weep with those who weep."
(Romans 12:15 NLT)

I tend to avoid conversations with people in my life who are pushy, aggressive, and unkind. Ask God to help you to have a gentler demeanor in all of your interactions. Ask Him to help you to be more soothing to those who are struggling, no matter what their struggle may be. Ask God to help smooth out your rough edges and allow you to possess more of a kind spirit all-around. Ask God to help increase in you so that your gentle character can allow others to see Him shining through you.

Sometimes an initial response to someone may come in the form of an aggressive comeback or a mean retort. It's a battle to be gentle when the flesh prods you to fight. However, someone who has been watering this Fruit of the Spirit will recognize that a gentle person knows when to let go and let God. Allowing God to deal with others so that we aren't tempted to take matters into our own hands.

Ask God to help you filter out the things that go from your mind to your mouth. Enable the Holy Spirit to help speak life through you and not death. Remember gentle people are not harsh, crude, or calloused.

> *"Those who control their tongue will have a long life; opening your mouth*
> *can ruin everything." (Proverbs 13:3 NLT)*

Although the nursery rhyme states that sticks and stones may break your bones but words can never harm you, this could not be more false. Words are like sharp knives, they can inflict wounds and make invisible cuts that bleed for a very long time.

Be purposeful and diligent with the words that come out of your mouth. Know that your actions and what you speak to others has a lot more power than you may originally have believed. Do not be flippant with your speech, because you never know when your blunt honesty might brutally wound someone that you care for.

> *"The tongue has the power of life and death…" (Proverbs 18:21 NIV)*

Someone in my life is very critical of me. They are constantly voicing their unsolicited opinions and judgments regarding my life. Because of our family tie, they believe they have the right to speak this way towards me. However, the problem I have always had with this isn't the advice that's being given, it's the manner with which it's being thrown at me.

We have had this very debate about gentleness more times than I can count. That the opinions expressed towards me are valid and allowed, but that it needs to be done in a kind and gentle manner. These interactions have been a continuous sore spot that has really bothered and rubbed me the wrong way. I have had to decompress in many counseling sessions because of the ongoing hurt these types of interactions have on my heart. And through these frustrating experiences, I have learned just how truly important being gentle is.

We can disagree with our brothers and sisters in Christ, and God even calls us to call them out in love. But the key here is to call them out GENTLY.

I will respect an opinion that is different from my own, as long as it is being expressed in a gentle manner. People disagree, moral compasses combat at times, and hard discussions are sometimes inevitable.

The best way to be able to discern if both you and the person you are having a discussion with are walking with the Spirit, is to observe whether you are able to debate something with a gentle demeanor.

Gentle means not yelling. Gentle means not manipulating. Gentle has no room for cussing or name calling. Gentle does not need a tone.

Gentle is respectful and patient. Gentle is enduring and persevering. Gentle has boundaries and a voice, but that voice comes charged by the Spirit, not by the world. Gentle is having control over your emotions in the face of a raging storm, it is staying calm during adversity. Not allowing the world to sway or surrender your beliefs.

Jesus is described as being, "gentle and humble of heart." God wants your character to be portrayed in the very same manner.

Trust me on this one, you will get a lot farther in life by being gentle rather than abrasive. By choosing to be humble instead of prideful. By putting God's cause before your own selfish wants and desires. By tending to someone's wounds not with tough love, judging and cold towards someone's sins. But by exhibiting the love that Jesus has for each of us, by being comforting and loving. By speaking the truth in a gentle manner and from a soothing heart.

We are not to rub salt in the wound of someone who is already hurting. We are to kneel down, bandage them up, and help them to walk into the light. Our demeanor is an exact reflection of our faith. Allow the weary to yearn for the comforting embrace of Jesus. Not to feel afraid of the wrath of God when they are feeling so lost and unsure of themselves. Help lead the burdened to the one safe place they can lay their heads and rest.

"The gentle are blessed, for they will inherit the Earth."
(Matthew 5:5 HCSB

There is strength in gentleness. Contrary to what many think, it takes a supernatural strength to allow yourself to be unscathed by the burning fires of the world. The enemy shoots arrows of flames at our backs, hoping to brand us. To char our delicate skin, turning our porcelain flesh into something blistered and scarred.

By staying pure and gentle, in the storm that is our existence, we are showcasing the strength of God.

A New Harvest Is Near

Through the process of God growing and blossoming my faith, I have begun to cultivate a deep love for all living things. I have always been somewhat of a tree-hugger and animal aficionado, but my passions have only quadrupled over the years as I have walked out my faith.

Since moving to Portland, my husband and I have excitedly begun a garden. We grew corn, onions, cauliflower, tomatoes, and a variety of different flowers all in pots and containers over this summer. We were so delighted when our crops began to produce.

There's no feeling more satisfying than cooking a plant-based meal with vegetables grown from your very own hands!

However, being the cook that I am. I also yearned to have an herb garden filled with rosemary, basil, dill, thyme, mint, and so forth. We looked around, found a great deal, and purchased an AeroGarden for the kitchen. If you don't know what that is, let me explain. This is a fully functional, you-really-can't-mess-this-up, foolproof way of gardening. You get these little pods to put in the machine and then a light will blink when it is low with water or plant food, and an artificial sun-light will turn on for a few hours during the day and "Ta-da!" you have an entire herb garden with barely any work!

Nonetheless, I took great pride in my herb garden, trimming and cutting it almost daily so that it could grow big and strong. And huge it did grow, to the point that no matter how often I pruned, the plants were still spilling all over the place.

It was awesome to say the least!

However, when the Oregon wildfires ravaged our beautiful state, and the unbreathable air covered Portland like a thick blanket of polluted black smoke. An unexpected result happened - my beloved and cherished herb garden shriveled up and blackened. This seemingly happened overnight. One day I was making homemade vegan pesto and the next I was staring like a forlorn puppy at my mass of sooty dead plants. This destruction of life made me more melancholy than I expected.

Unknowingly, I had found so much joy cultivating my precious herbs, watching them grow from nothing but a seed to something massive and towering. Yes, I enjoyed the outdoor gardening too, but since it had been spider season for the last 2 months (yes, that is really a thing in Oregon, which let me tell you I had no idea about before moving here). Going outside and tending to our garden was more like a rescue mission: get out and get back inside before multiple gigantic spiders try to hitch a ride indoors through your hair. I wasn't brave enough to nurture and care for those plants as tenderly as I was with my inside herb garden.

I don't know why I didn't just clean it up. But I left those dilapidated dead herbs, decaying in that dang AeroGarden. Every time I went into the kitchen I got a little sad, thinking of the life and creation that I had so enjoyed growing. Jake could noticeably see my mood change whenever we would be having a conversation in the kitchen and my eyes would wander to my murdered plant babies. I'm embarrassed to admit that this went on for weeks.

And then, one morning like always, I trudged downstairs in my fuzzy socks and pink robe and entered the kitchen to pour myself a much-needed cup of steaming hot fresh black coffee. From the kitchen cupboard I grabbed a mug that had no pair, as I have this silly quirk where I like to drink out of matching coffee cups with Jake. And since he's the early-riser to my night-owl he always has his coffee before me. We buy our coffee cups in pairs, so each morning I match my cup with his.

Anyways, I walked over to the coffee maker, eyes still half-closed with grogginess and gasped aloud. I flipped on the light, just to make sure my sleepy vision had not betrayed me in the darkness of the kitchen.

There was my AeroGarden, positioned where it always was, yet there were no black plants falling out of it. There were only almost invisible to the eye, short stubs. My husband, being the wonderful man that God created him to be, decided to take matters into his own hands and snip and clean this area of death and decay in our kitchen.

Instantly, God hit me with a revelation. How are we as children of the Lord to be fertile soil to produce His fruit, if we hold onto the dead stuff in our lives?

I used to hold onto my past, and wear it on my shoulder like a badge of victimization, unwilling to forgive and let go of the things in my life that had hurt me so badly. My sins and past defined who I was, and I was scared to find out who I would be without them weighing me down.

When I decided to fully walk with the Lord and not just simply talk the talk, I was convicted to finally fully let go of my hurts, habits, and hang-ups.

You see, Jesus has already forgiven us for our sins. He wants to produce goodness in our lives.

Although my beloved herb garden had withered and died due to its unexpected circumstances (toxic ash-filled air), the soil could still be fertile and produce a new crop. But that feat would be impossible if I refused to let go of the failure that I had experienced with the first go-around.

In order to allow God to show his goodness, we have to allow our soil to be plowed and cleansed. The dead plants had to be cleared out, so that new life could spring up from their ashes.

Let The Crow Go

This is now my second time to mention crows in this book. Before moving to Oregon, crows were never on my radar. Like never. But now I am making many connections with these strange black beasts.

As I sit here staring out my window, I am watching as two crows are bullying a squirrel. They have flanked him on either side of the tall green grass in the yard. Every time the furry little squirrel (we'll call him Squirrely) tries to get away, they lunge towards him and make him retreat back to his small confinement on the lawn.

A part of me is tempted to go out there and shoo the bully crows away, but Stella is watching intently from her perch and this is the most action she's gotten in days, so I also really don't want to rob her of this unaccustomed joy.

But what this instance is reminding me of, is something I learned a while ago regarding crows. The crow is apparently the only bird that will peck at the majestic eagle.

Listen to this craziness: while the eagle is in flight, the crow will fly above it and perch itself on the massive eagle's back and bite its neck.

The eagle however doesn't respond or fight with the pesky crow that is invading its space and attempting to harm it. Instead, the mighty eagle spreads its wings and begins to soar vertically upward dramatically into the sky.

The higher the eagle flies, the harder it is for the crow to breathe. Eventually the crow must disengage, falling due to the lack of oxygen.

I loved both the imagery and the lesson that I learned from this. My husband especially did as well, because while I use the butterfly metaphor, he prefers to compare himself to an eagle.

The eagle does not become distracted from what it's doing just because it's being attacked by a crow. The eagle never ceases, becomes discouraged, or allows the crow to ruffle their feathers (pun intended).

Crows are all around us. And while I am not encouraging a prideful mindset of being better than others, it is important to recognize people who are either for you or against you. Individuals who are walking with God or walking away from Him.

Crows can also take the form of different temptations and tactics that the enemy uses to keep you flying low. To try and deter you from soaring to the expansive heights that you were designed to reach.

These crows can come in the form of addictions, like alcohol, pain killers, food, materialism, or even pornography. These crows could look like mental illness, such as depression, crippling anxiety, or PTSD. These crows could even come in the form of distractions like wayward codependent friends and toxic relationships.

There could even be crows in your life that are in your very family. Judgmental beings who have an opinion about everything that you do, who discourage or belittle the very things that you know God is calling you to walk out.

Like the crows that constantly cuss me out in their squawking bird language when I go on a "peaceful" walk or when I leave the house and have to quickly retreat to the safety of my car, these pesky creatures are everywhere.

They used to really bother me, both the real crows and the metaphorical ones. As a people-pleaser at heart, I would get so bogged down by others' opinions, that I would clog up my ears to the only opinion that actually mattered, the one of my Lord and Savior.

I wanted so badly for people to like me. To make others happy and proud. For someone, anyone, even a stranger I had never met, to find value in who I was and what I was doing. I wanted to feel worthy of approval. I wanted to feel like I was enough.

But I have learned the hard way, that if I allow my worth to be determined by silly human opinions and judgements, then I am doomed. I will never live up to my potential if I'm constantly allowing myself to get disturbed and distracted by the pecking of the crows.

Fly high baby.

Let God take you to heights you thought were unattainable. The only opinion that matters at the end of the day, comes not from this Earth but from Heaven. Think about it: the higher you allow your Lord to take you, the closer you will be to the glory of Heaven.

A therapist once told me something that has always stuck with me.

"Someone else's opinion of you is none of your business."

Wait what?!

That one threw me for a curve ball, but the longer I contemplated it, the more it began to ring true.

Who cares if you don't like what I am doing? That's a "you" problem. If I'm following God and He is leading my steps, then I know I'm good.

Who cares if others do not see the value in me? Jesus has shown me the tender love and worthiness that I know to be true about myself. And no one on Earth can rob that from me.

You want to peck at my wings? Go ahead. I have on God's armor and I am Holy Spirit charged. No person, drink, or depressing thought is going to rob this truth from me.

Keep on flapping your beautiful wings my sweet friend. Persevere through the attacks of today. You were meant to soar higher than those pesky crows.

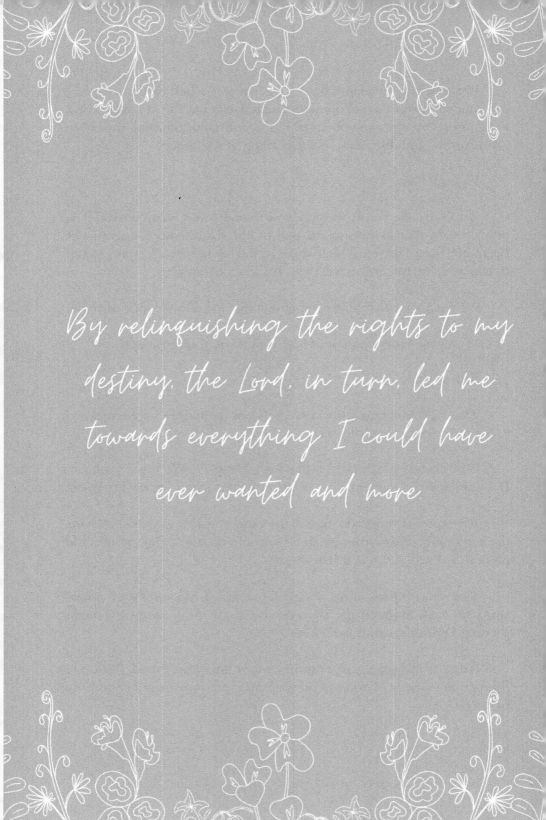

By relinquishing the rights to my destiny, the Lord, in turn, led me towards everything I could have ever wanted and more.

Self-Control

I don't know about you, but sometimes I just feel downright out of control. Especially in my past, as the uber-emotional being that I was created to be. Once my emotions hit, they took over. I would spiral down, into a deep hole, where it was dark and desolate.

I used to think that the solution to my emotional control was to take control of my own life. To take the power away from my sadness, unforgiveness, anger, or whatever emotion that was threatening to take over. It was so exhausting, I burned through dozens of self-help books and although I did learn some useful strategies, it still was never enough.

And that's because the fact of the matter was always right in front of me. I alone, am not enough. I can't masterfully control my life; it's too much for me to handle.

I can't do it alone.

When I submitted to my Master, and allowed Him to drive the vehicle of my life, everything just got so much better.

Self-control is the ability to keep your emotions and thoughts in check, instead of letting your feelings guide your life. It's having the knowledge that no matter the extenuating circumstance, you are still able to display discipline, temperance, and a calm demeanor. Self-controlled people allow God to guide them towards what is significant versus urgent, enabling us the ability to show restraint instead of enacting impulsive behavior.

God will help us to not make a mess of our lives by enabling us to practice discipline and self-control, even with our own emotions. Ask God to help you to tamper down and control your frustrations. Whether they be big or small does not matter, because we need to ask for help with it all.

> *"A man who does not control his temper is like a city whose wall is broken down." (Proverbs 25:28 HCSB)*

We need to learn to control our emotions and stop letting them take control of us. I could have saved myself so many problems and confrontations if I had just understood this simple lesson years ago. But instead of taking some deep breaths in the heat of the moment and praying for God to be with me during times of adversity, I would allow my emotions to take the wheel.

Inevitably, they would drive me and everyone around me, off a very steep cliff.

Let's be honest. Life is an emotional roller coaster sometimes. Okay I admit, most of the time!

Our emotions will be tested in many different situations. There are times when I start to get sad or upset, even when I really don't want to be. Recognizing my emotional state is one of the most important lessons that I have learned.

At first when I tried to train this part of the Fruit of the Spirit, I became very flustered and frustrated. I started to get angry and resentful when I started to feel an emotion that I did not want to be experiencing. But Jesus reminded me that He too dealt with anger, frustration, disappointment, and sadness.

The shortest verse in all of the Bible shows just how emotional Jesus became at times.

"Jesus Wept." (John 11:35 HCSB)

But the main difference between how Jesus handled His many emotions and how I handled mine was that Jesus took control of His emotions. He did not allow a strong feeling to dictate His thoughts, actions, or speech. He recognized the emotions He was having, as He was human and experienced all of the same feelings that we struggle with. But Jesus learned how to put a muzzle on the beast of His negative emotions.

I mean, sheesh, if I had people slandering my very name and trying to constantly sabotage, manipulate, and kill me, there is no way I would be able to be as calm and collected as Jesus was!

But our wonderful Christ, He is honored as The Prince of Peace for a reason.

Jesus did not allow the demoralizing things of the world or the discouraging human emotions that were weighing Him down to stop Him from doing the good work that He had set out to do. Emotions are inescapable - we humans were created to experience utter joy and also devastating destruction. Our emotions are what make our worship of the Lord so powerful and inspiring.

But we must practice and learn how to have self-control over our hundreds (okay, thousands) of varying emotions.

The enemy loves to distract you; that is his purpose. He lives to make you disheartened, to forget or get side-tracked and away from the plan that the Lord has for you. The enemy seduces us with different temptations, whether that be lust for power, money, sex, alcohol, food, drugs, possessions, or whatever it is. He whispers lies into our minds that we are useless, undeserving, a talentless failure that always was and will be. He uses these deceitful tactics so that he can trap us in our sin.

Become

This is where self-control comes in. We need to be diligent and disciplined in our walk with God. In filling our spirit with words of truth and light so when the enemy tries to steal, kill, and destroy our God-ordained missions, we know how to stand up to his lies and battle him out of our minds with scripture from God's living word.

This is why it's so important to walk along the path that the Lord has plowed for you. It's imperative that we put on our God armor every single day.

> *"This is why you must take up the full armor of God, so that you may be able to resist in the evil day, and having prepared everything, to take your stand. Stand, therefore, with truth like a belt around your waist, righteousness like armor on your chest, and your feet sandaled with readiness for the gospel of peace. In every situation take the shield of faith, and with it you will be able to extinguish all the flaming arrows of the evil one. Take the helmet of salvation, and the sword of the Spirit, which is God's word." (Ephesians 6:13-17 HCSB)*

My sweet husband wears a bracelet with this very verse on his wrist to remind him that every day he must don his armor, as if his life depended on it. Because it does!

My phone starts glitching out and not working properly when it's low on battery. Thus, I make sure that it's always charged and ready to aid me in whatever purpose I'm using it for. Think about this for a minute, every night we are very diligent in plugging our phones in before bed. This act of charging our devices has become such an ingrained habit, that many times I bet we do it without even thinking twice about it.

Your soul is a lot like your phone battery. In order to operate properly and to maximize your function-ability, you need to plug your spirit into God's word and charge up. Every day, we need to get in the word in one way or another. I am a firm believer of actually reading and studying the Bible. That doesn't mean that I don't love a riveting Christian memoir, in-depth Bible study, moving sermon, or motivating podcast. Heck, I love all of those!

But I also know that these facets with which I learn about the Lord are coming from human interpretation. In order to truly grow close to my Father and His Son, I need to dive into His living word. To open up my Bible and let Him speak directly through me, not through another person who then can impact me.

God wants to be intimate with each and every one of us. He wants us to learn to fine-tune our ears to His gentle voice.

Self-control is what helps to empower us to deny the allure of the world, to resist temptations, and control the lusts of the enemy.

In order to walk boldly with the Spirit, we must cultivate our self-control so that we will be able to stand strong and oppose the desires of our naturally sinful flesh.

> *"You took off your former way of life, the old self that is corrupted by deceitful desires; you are being renewed in the spirit of your minds; you put on the new self, the one created according to God's likeness in righteousness and purity of the truth." (Ephesians 4:22-24 HCSB)*

When we accept Jesus as our Lord and Savior and choose to be baptized, our old selves die; we are washed clean of our dirty sins. The cloth is white as snow, and we are made brand new. This is one of the reasons why I truly feel like my old self and my past are almost entirely different people and lives.

God cleansed us, creating a new creature from the ashes of our sin. And He wants us to act renewed also. As redeemed children, we are no longer to fall into the wayward habits of our dead worldly selves.

Self-control is essential to an obedient Christian life. Our flesh is full of destructive passions, finding pleasure in the soul-sucking temptations of this world. But by releasing the power of God into our lives, the Spirit will enable us to break through our old chains and walk into freedom with nothing holding us captive. It is time to live on a supernatural level, rejecting the flesh and respecting the Spirit.

"I say then, walk by the Spirit and you will not carry out the desires of the flesh." (Galatians 5:16 HCSB)

Hidden Beauty

On the first date I ever had with my husband, he said something to me that no one had ever said before. Something that struck me to my core, and made me look at both myself and my circumstances in a different perspective. Since we had met at Celebrate Recovery, there was obviously a discussion to be had regarding why we were both attending those meetings at the church.

You see, Celebrate Recovery is a Christ-centered recovery program that is aimed at anyone who struggles with sorrow, pain, or addiction of any kind. It is aimed to help you work through your hurts, habits, and hang-ups while putting Jesus at the center of your life. It's a safe place, where you can not only find freedom from the issues that are controlling you, but you can also find a God family that gives you a sense of purpose, community, and acceptance.

However, when the inevitable subject came up regarding why I was attending, my hands began to shake and I started to feel a nervous hot-flash come over me. Never before had I been so upfront and raw about my past struggles.

Here sat before me, what in my eyes, I can only describe as a living Michelangelo sculpture. He was so beautiful both inside and out. Although only knowing one another for a brief time, my spiritual gift of discernment told me all I needed to know about his heart.

I was scared of telling this intriguing man about my past. Fearful of what he would think of me. Betting that he would just throw up both of his hands and exclaim, "Yeahhhh, not interested. You're too much of a mess to take on. Not worth it."

Telling him about my past with alcohol addiction and abuse was like lifting up my sleeve and pant leg and showing him the permanent scars riddling my body from the bones I had broken during my childhood. Although those scars were always with me, most of the time they were overlooked and undetected. An ugly part of myself that I neither displayed or made known.

In the past, I have struggled (a lot) with honesty. Being guilty of glossing over important details, manipulating perceptions, and making myself appear more put together than I actually was. But in that moment, as my head was already instinctively formulating a story of a prettier version of the real me, the Holy Spirit stirred, encouraging me to be honest. To be real, to openly display my internal scars, and allow myself to be vulnerable.

So for the first time in my life, I was completely honest about my struggles and sins. About my past and about where God was leading me. About my journey on sobriety, on growing closer to the Lord, and on healing through Christian counseling from my past hurts.

After finishing, there was a quiet pause on his end. And then he said, "You have got to be the most disciplined woman I have ever encountered."

I was shocked; I quite literally had no words. And that's not a normal occurrence, to say the least! My mouth turned up into the most genuine smile without even realizing it, and we both just looked at each other happily, knowing that our meeting was most definitely God-ordained.

God worked through Jake to help me understand that although I had made many mistakes and been through quite a bit of adversity, it had produced in me a strong spirit of self-control. I had learned to stay disciplined in what the Lord was trying to work through me, and I had become a more determined and dedicated Christian because of my past.

Let Go And Let God

It's important to note that there is a major difference between "self-control" and simply the singular word "control". Control is something that many women, myself included, struggle with. As managers of the daily household, we inadvertently assume a role of control over what goes on in our families lives.

We are typically the ones shopping for, planning, and cooking the meals. The house only truly gets deep cleaned when we plan for it. When there is a trip, holiday party, or outing of any sort, we are typically the ones in charge of making sure the road trip snacks are in the backseat, Nana's present is wrapped nicely with a card that everyone has signed, and the hiking shoes are in the trunk of the car in case we decide to randomly go on an adventure.

It is both a satisfying and stressful feeling to know that there is so much riding on our preparation and careful planning for the family to continue to function without many bumps in the road. Inadvertently, we have had to assume some level of control in regards to the daily functioning of our families, thus this feeling of need for control can very easily trickle into many other areas of our lives.

It even blatantly says back in the book of Genesis, after the great fall of Adam and Eve, that Eve would forever struggle with control. And boy, do I feel that. I don't by any means intend to be controlling in things, but sometimes I struggle with just letting go and letting God.

I can't plan out everything, thus I should really stop trying to. It's not up to me how many little kiddos we have one day. But you best believe, I still have my preference of two boys and two girls and also have each and every one of their names, including middle, picked out (with Jake's approval of course).

The funny thing is, I am sooooo not in control of that! God has all the power, and rightly so. He will decide how many children he wants our family to have and He will gift us with whatever genders go best with His plan for our family. Yet, like a little girl who has been told "no" multiple times to having a cookie, I still struggle with wanting what I want.

I used to have this very rebellious motto for my life. "I do what I want, when I want, how I want."

Lordy, can you imagine how much of a handful I used to be?!

God's Plan Is Sovereign

I have to admit something to ya'll. I have a girl crush. Okay, maybe more like a role model admiration.

I love Christine Caine. There, I said it!

I think she is such a bold warrior for God's Kingdom, and I look up to her immensely. I remember the first time I ever heard her speak, I was attending my childhood church Celebration in the slow-paced town of Georgetown, Texas. The lead pastor announced that we would have a guest speaker that day, and out walked Christine, jubilant as ever, skipping to the beat of her own drum. I was only nine at the time, but something in my heart was struck and has never been the same since. Christine had a riveting message that day, with much of it centered around sex trafficking.

As a young little thing, I had no idea what that was. But after her explanation, I wept with emotion for women and children I had never met. My heart hurt knowing that these atrocities were occurring on a regular basis right then (and yes, still right now). Since that day, I have had a fire in my soul for helping to rescue women and children from this atrocious form of modern-day slavery.

In 8th grade we had to do a research paper on any subject of our choosing. I chose to do mine on human trafficking. Each student was to read their paper aloud in front of the class. However, before the presentations my teacher pulled me aside and said that although my paper was very well written and researched, that it was not appropriate to read in front of the class. I balked, angry and confused. He explained that this material could be very upsetting to the other children, and he did not want to subject them to having to hear about something so brutal.

That very day, I made a vow to never stop talking about human trafficking. To never again let the war cry in my heart be silenced because it was "uncomfortable" or "hard to digest". Heck yeah it's hard to digest the fact that children younger than kindergarteners are being used as sex slaves! But this horror isn't just happening in third-world countries like many might initially believe, this is happening right here on our very own soil.

My classmates that day should have heard my speech; they should have been made aware of something that they themselves could fall prey to. Since that eye-opening day in middle school, at almost every opportunity where a research paper or speech was needed, I wrote about human trafficking.

In my Senior year in college at Texas A&M University I really dove into this passion again, and endeavored to get more involved. I was working hard towards being fully sober, had started attending AA meetings and accountability groups on campus, and was even going weekly to a counselor who was aiding my efforts on this journey. Through my internship writing for a local newspaper, I was assigned to write an article over human trafficking efforts in the area.

After speaking with the founder of the Human Trafficking and Exploitation Action Network, my passion was reignited. I wanted to full force, get involved. I joined the board of directors, reignited my efforts by talking to others about Christine Caine's A21 organization and decided that I wanted to work for her and do her in-depth internship.

At this time, I was absolutely convinced that my next necessary step in life was to take some time off after college and intern for A21 for 6 months. I wanted to go work in the nitty gritty, in one of the rehabilitation centers for rescued human trafficking victims. I wanted to dive in deep and go to Greece and work in one of the biggest human trafficking cities in the world. I was convinced that this was where I needed to be. I applied and prayed very hard over this.

When I made it to the second round of interviews I stalled out a little, because it was my last semester of finals at the time but then I got everything submitted and continued to pray over the acceptance of my application. If I were to get accepted, I would be leaving in the middle of the summer and stay in Greece until January of the next year. I was so excited!

After graduation, I still had not heard back so I got myself a remote content writing job and began to save the pennies that I made to prepare for this trip. I moved back to Austin, although I did not feel ready to come back to my hometown and waited - very impatiently, might I add.

Finally, the day came, when I was informed that I was not chosen for Christine Caine's internship. I was devastated. Dark looming thunderous clouds rolled in on the hot summer day we were suffering through in Texas.

I felt at a total loss, not knowing up from down. That internship was the only direction that felt to be the right path. It was the one thing I was counting on. I truly did not know what to do with myself.

Eventually I took my grievances to the Lord, and we had it out. I was upset because I felt this whole passion for human trafficking was God-led, and let me tell you, I very blatantly expressed this anger towards Him. I acted like a bratty child, throwing a tantrum because she didn't get the Barbie she liked at the grocery store. Through the roller coaster of my tumultuous emotions, I got the feeling of God speaking to me.

He asked me, "Do you want to be in control of your life, or would you like me to be?"

That simple question right there stunned me silent. I thought back to all the times that I had taken "control" of my life and shuddered with memories of past regrets and mistakes. No, I most definitely did **not** want to be in control of my life. I desperately needed God to guide me, to gently steer me in the right direction, because time and time again I had proven that I just wasn't capable of that feat on my own.

The Lord spoke to me to armor up, to be prepared. I had absolutely no idea what that meant, but I made sure to not take His guidance lightly. Once again, I began seeing a Christian counselor. I began praying more than ever for my weary heart to be tended to, and for direction to be introduced into my life.

I got myself an additional part-time job on top of the content writing and began to save up. I started confiding with some Christian mentors who helped to guide me on my journey towards healing, forgiveness, and growing closer in my walk with the Lord. It was recommended to me to go to Celebrate Recovery.

At the time, although I was praying every day and admittedly crying daily about how lost I felt on my journey, I was still stubbornly trying to fit God into the white space of my life. I was still trying to intertwine Him where it was most comfortable and convenient for me.

An image always comes to mind when I think back to how I was during that time of my life. It was like I had my hands outstretched in front of me, palms up towards the Heavens, but my fists were both tightly clenched closed. I was demanding that God lead me, and guide me toward more calm waters, yet I was unwilling to unclench my fists and give Him my hands.

Finally, I got to the point where I humbled myself, and in my mind I "unclenched" my fists but in God's eyes all I really did was outstretch my thumb and pointer finger from its casing, still enclosing the last three fingers on my hands tightly shut.

At that time, I was very alone in my walk with sobriety, healing, and Christ. My "friends" were all extremely lost and users of one sort of drug or another. Thus, the first time I went to Celebrate Recovery (CR for short) I went on a night that was convenient for me, and drove out of city limits to go there. It was a very good experience, but it was daunting walking in alone, being the youngest thing in the room and probably being one of the most messed up. That first experience with CR was a little too real for me; it made me feel extremely raw and vulnerable. Thus, being the coward I was, afraid of having the lights turned on to expose all of my sins hiding out in the dark, I did not go back the next week.

However, God kept poking and prodding at me. He wanted me to fully open up my fists. He wanted to take my hand and guide me towards His plan and glory for my life.

The next few weeks got very dark for me. I would cry most days with an overwhelming feeling of devastation and lost-purpose drowning my soul. At this point in my life, I felt so low that when I would wake up in the morning, I would get sorrowful at having to endure another day.

Finally, through my depression and in the midst of my never-ending tears, I threw myself on the ground and yelled, "I give up! I don't want to control my life anymore. I NEED you Lord. Please save me. Please guide me. Your plan for my life is my plan. I will go wherever you want to lead me. I will do whatever you have intended for me to do. I am your servant and you are my Master. I give my everything to you. Please help me God."

In that moment, I humbled myself to my core. I metaphorically unlocked my stubbornly clenched fists and outstretched my hands high and wide towards the Heavens.

I surrendered everything I had, to my Heavenly Father.

And it was this turning point in my life that led me through a series of events to be here today, typing away on my laptop as my steaming cup of coffee aromatically comforts me, fulfilled and satisfied in the purpose the Lord has designed for me.

After that humbling moment, down on my knees, the only thing that kept persisting in my mind was to go to Celebrate Recovery again. To do so urgently, and not delay.

Originally I thought maybe I should go back to the CR that I had first attended, but that meeting was still a few days away and I felt a pressing sense of urgency. I already had obligations to watch a friend perform at a club that evening but the Holy Spirit prompted me to reconsider. I found myself canceling my plans for the event that I was to attend and searching for a CR that would take place that night instead.

I remember my heart racing, feeling a sense of nervousness as I raced towards the CR, as I was going to be late since I had been debating at the front door so long whether or not I should actually go. But ultimately God had commanded it, and I needed to be bold in my faith and follow wherever it was that He led me.

I remember parking my black convertible Mustang in the church parking lot of Grace Covenant. I had never attended church there before, but I always passed by the large building as I was driving towards my rented condo near the 360 Overlook.

I remember feeling like a lost puppy, trying to find its way home. I had no idea where to go, but then I saw the back of two tall figures walking through a set of double doors. I hurried after them, intending to ask them if they too were there for CR.

I nearly ran into the stopped pair, as I hustled quickly through the door. Embarrassed, I kept my eyes down and mumbled if either of them knew where CR was being held. The older one explained that they, too, were going to CR and were just waiting for the elevator. That I could ride up with them.

We waited there silently for a second, my eyes still downcast, as sometimes I can be uber awkward around strangers. In an attempt to get the conversation going, the older gentleman noted my refillable water bottle in my hand and exclaimed, "What is it with bringing those water bottles? Both of you have one!"

I looked down at my water bottle, made eye contact with the gent and stuttered, "Well, it's always good to stay hydrated."

The man standing next to the older one began to chuckle, "That's exactly what I said!"

And all of a sudden an outstretched fist was in front of me, I looked up at the tall towering man extending this gesture to me and my breath caught. Heat instantly rose to my face, my cheeks flushed pink, and all of a sudden I felt like I was in the Sahara Desert. The man smiling down at me was the most handsome creature I had ever set my eyes upon. He had large inquisitive brown eyes lined with thick dark lashes, his lips were set with an inviting smile, and just the look of him felt like home.

In that moment, I think I forgot how to breathe. I am sure I stood there for an awkwardly long amount of time with his fist outstretched, just gazing like a deer in the headlights. Luckily, eventually my muscle memory kicked in and I fist bumped him back. A simple gesture of camaraderie and friendship, yet it sent electric currents throughout my entire body.

We rode the elevator up and had some small talk. The pair found out that it was my first time at that CR and were very kind towards explaining the whole process to me. I was too busy being self-conscious and taking note of my appearance to kindly remind them that I had been to a CR before, just not this specific location.

Why had I worn zero makeup?! I totally didn't brush my hair today. OMG, did I seriously forget to wear a bra? Was the salsa stain that wouldn't come out of my light blue blouse too noticeable?

When the elevator door opened, I quickly retreated to the coffee bar mumbling something about how it was nice to meet them both. Ugh, I was such a mess. Of course the day that I encounter the most beautiful man in the universe, I look like something a truck ran over.

I wanted to stay as far away from them as possible, because I had come to that meeting for God and my sobriety. No way was I going to allow any distractions, especially tall handsome beautiful ones, to divert my attention. However, as I was making my cup of coffee, I felt a presence behind me.

"Hi again, since it's your first time here I was wondering if you wanted to sit with my Dad and I? It's never fun to sit alone." The man smiled a dazzling smile down upon me, and ya'll, my knees seriously wobbled. I meekly nodded, throwing my inhibitions out the window and followed him to a round white table with fold-up chairs surrounding it.

At Grace, they served dinner to the CR attendees. That evening they were serving Jason's Deli sandwich boxes. The intriguing man, who I found out was named Jake, had grabbed the last dinner box, and he kindly offered it to me when we sat down. I politely declined, but he persisted. Finally, I embarrassingly told him that I was allergic to gluten and didn't eat meat, so that it really was okay for him to enjoy it.

As the meeting started, Jake began to open his dinner box, meticulously inspecting the items inside with care. Little did I know that he was reading the ingredients list on all the items trying to figure out if they contained gluten. Finally, he slid over his chips and pickle, winking at me as he whispered, "These don't have meat or gluten so I hope you enjoy them."

Instantly my cheeks heated up, as this small kind gesture meant more to me than I could begin to describe. So many times in my life men had been incredibly selfish towards me, that I had just become used to it. But this perfect stranger was taking his time, and genuinely trying to be generous and hospitable. It made me send out an internal prayer, begging God that one day He would prepare a husband for me that was this considerate and kind.

As the evening came to a close and it was time to leave, I shoved away from my chair quickly. Trying to escape from the extremely distracting man that had been sitting to my left. Wishing to flee from him, because in my heart I begrudgingly had concluded that men like him would never go for messes like me.

However, Jake chased after me calling my name! I turned back towards him not wanting to make eye contact again and he simply held out his hand in a cordial gesture saying it was a pleasure to meet me. I shook his hand and when I did he slipped a folded up piece of paper inside my palm.

I was too dumbfounded at his smoothness, that I embarrassingly crumpled the paper into my jean pocket and looked up at him. He simply smiled warmly at me and repeated how nice it was to meet me. I walked to my car feeling my cheeks burning and quickly unfolded the paper he had given me.

It read, "Your new friend in Christ, Jake Panko" with his number written below.

The largest smile I have ever had filled my face and I felt God very clearly speak to my heart that Jake was the man that He had designed for me.

That same evening I called my best friend and exclaimed, "I just met my future husband!" She of course dismissed me and laughed, like I was joking. But I just knew.

It's like being a locked door and lighting up when you encounter the key that was designed to open you. Somehow I knew, after that one brief encounter, that I would never be the same.

That I had met the person that God had created me for. That this man, this handsome specimen, was mine, and always had been.

The moral of this story is two-fold.

One, if God had allowed me to get accepted to that internship in Greece, I would never have met my precious husband. We would not have encountered each other at the critical time that we did in one another's lives.

At a time when we were both so lost in the raging sea of the world. God found us drowning and struggling, rescued us, and blessed us each by putting us together in the same rescue raft. If *my* plan for my life had played out, I would have missed out on the best gift that has ever been bestowed upon me.

Secondly, if I had never relinquished the control that I so badly wanted to have over my own destiny, I would never have found myself at that very CR that specific night. I would have continued on a lukewarm Christian path, slowly making my way towards the truth, but seemingly for every step forward taking two more unsure steps back in the wrong direction.

When many people think of self-control they think of not doing something that they are tempted with, not partaking in a certain sin. While yes, this is one aspect of self-control. I do not find this to be all that there is to learn about this portion of the Fruit of the Spirit.

Self-control is recognizing either the enemy's influence or your own pride within yourself and refusing to let it control you. It is humbling yourself to a point where you know you can't do whatever it is you are setting out to do without God's guidance. It is becoming less, so that you can make room for Jesus to become more through you.

Life will be filled with innumerable temptations, and many times the tempting thing looks like the more fun option in that moment. There were many instances of self-control that led up to the precious interaction that God allowed me to have with my future husband.

Had I not had self-control to become sober a year prior, I would have never even set foot in a Celebrate Recovery. Had I not had self-control to humble myself on my knees before the Lord and lean on Him for strength and guidance, I would not have allowed Him to lead me to one of the most life-altering moments of my existence. Had I not had self-control to say no to what was more "fun" I would have been at a venue that night dancing to blasting music, flashing lights, and surrounded by a room full of lost sinners.

There were a million tiny decisions that collectively culminated in order for Jake and I to meet under the house of the Lord.

Submitting to the Lord and enacting my self-control through the Spirit, led me to the man that was specifically created to love me. What a beautiful realization that is, that by relinquishing the rights to my destiny, the Lord, in turn, led me towards everything I could have ever wanted and more.

Your War Cry

We must stop avoiding change, stop fearing something that is so miraculous. Be brave and allow God to do a great work in you.

We must each be purposeful in our prayers, asking God to do whatever he needs to do in us so that we can exhibit His Fruit.

We must stop making excuses, running and hiding like little girls, afraid of the dark. Change is wonderful. And change is very essential in order for you to live up to the destiny you were created to fulfill.

You are more than capable of this transformational change, so long as you allow the Holy Spirit to propel you toward it. The Fruit of the Spirit becomes part of us when we walk in obedience to the Spirit.

Do you make excuses? Do you victimize yourself? Do you say, "I wish I could be as strong as you, but I just could never do that." Or exclaim, "I can't do that because I suffer from this or am diagnosed with that. You just don't understand what I have gone through."

You're right, I might not fully understand. But do you know who does?

Jesus.

He suffered way more than your abusive past or struggle with cancer. Jesus experienced depression, anxiety, anger, rejection, and abuse of the most malicious kind.

I don't say this to invalidate your feelings or the things you have suffered through. But I have been around the block enough with both myself and many of my friends regarding this topic.

And I am sick and tired of us all victimizing ourselves!

Life is hard, and it downright sucks at times. Relationships turn toxic and abusive, health incidents happen, finances wreck us, temptations steal our innocence, the list goes on and on and on. We live in a fallen world. But just because you've been stomped on, doesn't mean you have to assume the role of a kicked puppy all your life.

Get up!

Get off the ground. Climb out of that dark pit you believe you're stuck in. Rock bottom just means the only place to go from where you are - is up! I personally hit rock bottom more than once, but every time I got out of it. Not because I'm some superhuman with no emotions or empathy towards my misfortunes and circumstances. Quite the opposite actually, as I'm an extremely emotional being. But I prevailed because I gave my problems to God. They were too big for me to handle.

I refused to let the enemy win over my soul. Jesus had paid the ultimate price for ME and I was going to make sure that I didn't prove it to be a waste.

I'm sorry sweet sister for the hurt you have endured. I truly am.

I'm sorry for the people who have hurt you and the unfairness that has come your way. But you need to dry your tears and stop feeling sorry for yourself and the parts of yourself that have gotten hurt. You were created to be both gentle and strong. To be resilient and lovely. Not one or the other. We women are made to be Warrior Princesses. Graceful, kind, and loving, while also knowing how to fight the good fight and battle for what is right.

We are not a damsel in distress waiting to be saved. Girlfriend, believe me when I say no man can do that for you! But you do have a Prince, and His mighty name is Jesus. He is your Prince of Peace and He has already rescued you, even if you haven't yet accepted that fact and allowed it to heal your heart.

Let us encourage the women of today to stand strong, even through pain and adversity. They need to see you dip into the never-ending powerhouse of Heaven and allow God to fuel your strength and fire within your soul.

We each have some of that Heavenly Light residing inside of us, just waiting to burst out and shine brilliantly. I promise you, God can fulfill your dreams much better than you can.

In order to truly become who you were created to be, you have to relinquish control. You have to let go of all of the labels you have confined yourself with. Each worldly label that you have believed about yourself is a metal bar, within the cage that you are trapped in.

Take the bars down, now.

Depression is a metal bar - knock it down. PTSD is a bar. Obesity is a bar. Addiction is a bar. Anxiety is a bar. Busyness is a bar. Unworthiness is a bar. Ugly is a bar. Unemployed is a bar. Single is a bar.

KNOCK. THEM. DOWN.

Break free from the cage the enemy has seduced you to entrap yourself in. All of the negative words that you think about yourself ARE LIES.

All of the diagnoses from doctors are just labels a person from the world is giving you. Don't give them more power than they deserve. Just because you struggle with ADHD, does not mean that it should define you. Just because you have OCD, does not mean that you should use it as a crutch to forever cripple who you were meant to become.

The list goes on and on. This world is filled with sickness, whether that manifests in your life as spiritual, emotional, mental, or physical. The sad fact of the matter is that you will experience some form of it at one point or another.

Mental illness is very real. Just as much so as physical illness. But that doesn't mean you should allow it to define you. I struggle with depression and anxiety, but that's not my identity. I have PTSD, but I don't associate myself with that label.

I am Madison Avery Panko, a child of God, a Warrior Princess of the Highest King. Anointed to share my testimony to spread God's light and love.

Now, who are you?

Because I know for a fact that God has something grand in store for you. I know that if you allow Him to show you, and follow where He wants to lead you, you will never look back. This is one of the best decisions you could ever make and commit to.

Let your Lord give you a new name. Let Him anoint you with your true purpose.

It's time to escape from the cage the world has tried to put you in.

Don't let words define who you are. No one can trap you any longer.

Time To Put In The Work

Self-discipline and anointing go hand in hand.

I have always known I have been anointed to write, but only now, in my mid-twenties, am I beginning to walk out and explore that process.

I feel like so many of us believe that if it's in God's will, then it will be easy. Understand this sister, God doesn't do it for you. That's why He created you to fulfill that very specific purpose!

He will guide us and enable us to complete a great work for Him, but He doesn't just wave a magic wand and poof, I'm a best-selling author. Poof, I am up speaking next to the women that I have looked up to and learned from for years. Poof, I get to minister and speak to women who have struggled through the very things that, at one point in my life, I thought would break me.

I have to cultivate this craft that God has given me. I have to prove to God that I will go the distance for Him (insert song from Disney's *Hercules*). That I will work hard and then work even harder to do what He has commanded of me.

Our lack of discipline and diligence is very disappointing to Jesus. Think of our sweet Prince, He had more self-control than I can even imagine possessing. He stayed fighting the good fight, even when His very life was on the line.

Prepare yourselves. Show up in excellence and self-control.

You are not always going to feel motivated or inspired towards grinding for your purpose. I was very naive in this misunderstanding for a long time.

"Well, if it's in God's will, then it will be easy."

Wrong.

"If God wants me to do it so bad then I will wake up every day with motivation and inspiration."

Wrong again, sweet child.

You see, when God speaks to me, He always calls me sweet child. I don't fully understand why that is His name for me, but I do know that even as a young girl I have always been too big for my britches. In a rush to grow up, I was usually the first of my friends to do something. With that way of living, I lost my innocence towards life while still an adolescent. And now years later, I am trying so hard to get back to my roots of having a childlike heart. Of seeing the world without my jaded pessimistic glasses on.

God's name of endearment towards me helps to remind me that no matter how grown I become, I will always remain His child. Not a child that He has to scold and constantly disciple (although let me tell you I have been disciplined by God and that was NOT fun) but His sweet child, so that I can be reminded that I am loved, cherished, and treasured.

I am precious to God. And so are you.

Some days I wake up and the birds are chirping and the sun is shining (except not, because my favorite days are when it's pouring down rain) and I hop out of bed ready to write my heart out.

And other days I open my laptop and stare at my blank document for literally hours. Trying to drum up anything that doesn't sound like a 3rd grader wrote it.

Walking in your purpose is not always easy. Actually, I would say that it's one of the hardest things you might ever do. Especially in the beginning.

Greatness isn't given, it's earned.

We must learn to put one foot in front of the other. To show up every single day for God. To be diligent and determined.

I have always been good at winging it. That's actually when I shine best. But God wants to train me on how to prepare. How to work toward a goal and watch it come to fruition.

In my youth, I could get away with these impromptu tactics, but now God is convicting me to go to work for Him.

I want to break generational curses, and have my children reap the harvest of the seeds that I have toiled over planting.

The ability to choose what you want in the future, versus what you want right now, will set you immensely apart from others.

Don't you want to shine for God's Glory?

There is a need in the world for your very talents and God wants you to meet it.

Sometimes we are so distracted by what other people are doing that we don't step into the position that we need to. We don't focus on the mess we have made and need to clean up.

I'm not very good at structure. I have been called a free spirit all my life. However, I am coming to grips that I need to alter my ways. Organization, responsibility, and discipline is how we best are able to thrive with the Lord.

It's going to take longer than you thought. You need endurance. This is not an instant gratification gig.

Stop being too busy for God.

There is a generation coming after you and they are going to look to you to see where God is showing up. The making of a leader is not the ones that have never been hurt, it's the ones that have gotten up and kept going.

A leader is a person who picks themselves up off the battlefield and keeps marching forward.

The Lord is my strength. The Lord is my Shepherd. With God by my side, there is nothing to fear.

Comprehending Catastrophe

My mind is still kind of whirling. I'll be honest, I think I am in shock. There are so many different things that are racing through my head, I've given myself a migraine just trying to process it all.

I don't know if you would be interested to know, but this book wasn't going to be my first book. It honestly wasn't even in my realm of ever being a book. I was working on a fiction 3-part book series, a dystopian sci-fi novel, filled with action and entertainment. But as I was reading the very first chapter of *Lioness Arising,* God spoke to me and said, "You are the next generation of the coming."

It was such a clear instruction that He has anointed me with this gift to write and that I should dedicate my first book to Him and Him alone.

Enter *Become.* A book conceived by God himself.

As a woman who has struggled with anxiety for most of my life, instantly I began to stress out because I had done no planning for the book. Typically, I like to know exactly where my story is going to take my readers. I like to have a timeline, chapters outlined, and a rough idea as to what shape a project is going to take on. It was like I had fresh clay in front of me, completely untouched and utterly unmolded.

"God met me more than halfway, he freed me from my anxious fears."
(Psalms 34:4 MSG)

Then Jesus sweetly spoke to my heart. He reminded me of the verse that had become so near and dear to my soul. He helped to guide me on how this book would come to fruition, and the best way to set it up.

Jesus encouraged me to begin immediately, with a sense of urgency rising up inside of myself.

I can't quite explain this urgency to you. But it felt like there was no choice in the matter. That I *needed* to make this book. That this very conglomerate of pages that you are now holding, was somehow of dire importance. I sensed that I must stop everything else that I was doing and work on this immediately until it was finished.

I did not understand the hot fire that was lit under my booty by the Holy Spirit. But boy, could I feel it burning.

My husband was even surprised, questioning why writing this book right this very moment had taken top precedence over everything. All I knew at the time was that God wanted me to dive in deep with Him, Jesus, and the Holy Spirit to work on this book together.

Yesterday, the curtain was finally pulled back and I was able to understand why this book is so important. Why I needed to make it my life's work at the very period of time in my life that I did.

This book has served as a rock for me during yet another season in my life that is filled with struggle.

But before I explain that all to you, I think I had better back up a little bit and tell you about how good our God is.

The Beginning

For the past few years I have had this predisposition that something was wrong with my body. I just felt, deep down, that I was unhealthy in a way that I couldn't quite put my finger on.

I was eating right, active, and really working to eradicate all chemicals from my everyday life, yet something was still off. I went to visit many doctors and specialists, hoping to find a medical professional who would take my premonitions seriously, who would believe the symptoms I was having to be a small part of a possibly bigger problem.

I had the strongest inclination that it had something to do with my thyroid, that there was just something that wasn't right. Each time I would visit a different western medicine professional (your typical doctor or specialist) they would do my bloodwork, everything would come back in the normal range, and then they would say to me in more or less words, "Well maybe you are just stressed out or tired. Get some extra rest, I'm sure you'll feel better soon."

This would always infuriate me, making me feel both belittled and hopeless. I grew up through abuse, I was an alcoholic who struggled with addiction for many years, I had already lived through more stress than some people ever encounter. The stresses that have occurred in the past two years of my life have been nothing compared to my first two decades of life!

I began to feel like maybe I was going crazy. Maybe I was a hypochondriac and it was all in my head. Maybe I should just stop trying to have someone find an ailment that obviously wasn't there.

And for a while, the taunting lies in my head from the enemy persuaded me to give up searching. However, the Lord was not done with me yet. I kept feeling the Holy Spirit guiding me that I needed to move to Portland, Oregon. I began to express this to my husband and although I could not explain why I felt that God was calling us across the country, I just knew that we had to go and make haste. Finally, my husband conceded, trusting my spiritual discernment and we left all of our friends and family - virtually everything we had known our entire lives - and moved.

We arrived in Oregon, a large moving truck in tow, in the middle of March 2020. COVID-19 had just hit our nation, and during the lockdown my quality of life was very low.

Although we were in a new stunning place, surrounded by nature and all I wanted to do was prance around on a mountaintop and sing "The Hills are Alive" from *The Sound of Music*, my aching body kept me glued to the couch, and many months went by in a blur of both crying and sleeping.

My neck began to hurt very badly around that time. At first I hoped that maybe it was a simple cold, where your glands become enlarged and your lymph nodes get tender and swollen. But as the months went by and the pain began to worsen, the Holy Spirit reminded me of my thyroid. He spoke very clearly to me that I need not give up searching for an answer.

Jake and I had a difficult conversation, because I strongly felt that regular doctors were not doing their jobs sufficiently with giving me the care I needed. I was convicted that I needed to search for a medical professional who would take me as seriously as I believed I needed to be. We knew that this route, the path of finding and working with a naturopath would be very expensive, as natural medicine doctors are not typically covered by insurance.

My husband, however, had to trust in me and give credence to how strongly I discerned something being very wrong with my body. Ultimately, Jake told me that no amount of money was too much if it meant that I could recover my strength and heal from this mystery ailment. He wanted me to have a better quality of life, and I wanted more than anything to be the best wife that I could be. The type of wife that I had been striving to be, but was too fatigued to do a proper job at.

It was a large step of faith because in a time of financial strain with only one of us in the household having a steady job, we had to make the decision of whether or not we could afford this route. But we know from experience that God delivers, that He provides, and that He will take care of us financially no matter what. So we obeyed His command to keep trying, and I began the daunting task of finding a naturopath.

As a journalism major I went into "expert researcher" mode. I spent hours trying to figure out what all of my symptoms could mean. I learned about so many different bodily processes that my mind was constantly swimming with information. After I compiled all of that information, I then began to list out all of my symptoms.

After all was said and done, I had typed up a 6-page document listing out all of my symptoms, my complete medical history since birth, the ailments I suspected that could be possible, the testing I thought necessary to do, and my treatment plan goals.

I then interviewed almost a dozen of the best naturopaths in Portland, explaining my symptoms, learning about each doctor, and waiting for the Holy Spirit to give me the green light on which one would be the best to work with. It was a long process and very frustrating, as I was nervous about the possibility of picking a naturopath, spending an obscene amount of money, and then still getting nowhere.

Every naturopath that I interviewed was both stunned and impressed with my knowledge on the subjects that we were discussing. However, the Holy Spirit did not give me any indication of who I should work with until I met with Dr. Walker.

Many naturopaths will give you a free consultation. Because of COVID restrictions, most of these consultations occurred over the phone or via Zoom. However, one doctor in particular was interested in meeting me and doing an in-person consultation.

I remember clearly walking into her office, my bulging self-made packet in hand. I sat down in front of her and handed her my 6-page typed and bulleted document of symptoms and possible suspected ailments, us both trying to size one another up despite the masks, as she explained to me that we had only minutes together. That a good way to think of this consultation was to view it like speed dating. That I should do my best to explain to her everything that was going on, in the short allotted time that the consultation allowed.

She asked if I was ready, and I nodded, feeling the sweat of my hands drip down onto my jeans. She hit the timer and I was off. I don't really remember what all I said during that time, but man, was I on fire.

The Holy Spirit was working through me because I explained everything perfectly, articulated medical jargon professionally, and when the timer beeped the doctor just sat back in silence for a moment.

Finally, she reeled forward and clapped her hands together exclaiming, "Wow! That was the best speed date I have ever had in my entire career!"

She asked to see the document that I had brought, as she truly appreciated the determination I had towards getting better, and said that she could not just simply spend the allotted 15-minutes with me. That day we ended up talking for over an hour. She really took me seriously and I could tell that she genuinely valued the time, energy, and effort that I had dedicated towards trying to best explain my mystery ailments.

For the first time in years, I felt an overwhelming rush of peace regarding a doctor. The Holy Spirit was encouraging me that I could trust this woman, that she would be very thorough, and that I needed to schedule an actual appointment with her immediately.

So I left her office on her schedule for her earliest available appointment the next week, a smile on my face and a renewed determination towards becoming the best healthy self that I could be.

Our first appointment together was very detailed. Since I had so many different symptoms there were many different routes that we could go about with testing. Each different test would be a separate out-of-pocket cost, and the total was pretty astronomical if I wanted to do all of the testing upfront.

Humbly, I knew that our family just couldn't afford that. I wanted to get better, but I also wanted to be as frugal and cost efficient as I could while seeing such an expensive doctor.

Out of all of the avenues that she wanted to check out, I was still dead set on putting my thyroid first. I wanted that to be prioritized. The pain in my throat area had gotten to the point where as each day progressed I had to lower my voice to a whisper or stop talking altogether. I knew something was not right, and I wanted to get to the bottom of it.

Out of all the testing that she suggested, I decided that the first we should go with was an ultrasound on my thyroid and an at-home cortisol test to see if my adrenal glands were functioning properly. You see, the thyroid and the adrenals work symbiotically so if one is not working properly then it will have an impact on the other.

Although there were many other in-depth tests that she wanted to do and that I agreed would be valuable, the Holy Spirit was pushing me towards picking the two that we decided upon.

Going to the hospital alone to get the ultrasound was a bit daunting. I usually am never nervous about these things, as I have broken many bones and have been to the hospital for health issues more times than I can count.

As I lay there on the cold unforgiving surface, having the silent technician do the ultrasound, I just kept repeating in my head, "The Lord is my strength. The Lord is my Shepherd."

The technician captured images of the ultrasound in silence, and my anxiety was through the roof. When we were finished all she said was that she was going to send the images for further testing and that I should hear back in a few weeks.

A few weeks?!

I politely explained to her that I was a woman of faith, and that I needed to know if there was something that showed up that I should be praying about. She tried to mask her face as unconcerned as possible, while explaining to me that she wasn't allowed to give her opinion. I pressed a little further and finally she said, "Praying wouldn't hurt."

I left the hospital that day with a lump in my throat (literally and figuratively), as I think I already knew but was not allowing my mentality to go where my body had already ventured.

Jake and I had been praying over the results both hoping to find something and not to find something that was *too* serious. Today, I walked into my follow-up appointment with my naturopath fully knowing we would go over the results of all these tests. I put on my armor of God spiritually, and physically donned my favorite eccentric jacket purchased at Goodwill for $5, as I always felt better (and warmer) when wearing it.

My discernment had been spot on, and my body was indeed sick. It had not been functioning the way it should have been for a very long time now. I had been right all along, but since no doctor was willing to take me seriously, they had refused to do the extremely in-depth testing that would have yielded this conclusive outcome.

Since God encouraged me to me to not give up, I had faith that eventually something would be discovered, that one day I would finally get some concrete answers so that I could begin to heal my body and live with a better quality of life.

Our body is a temple with which we are to use to worship God. My temple had been crumbling, completely dilapidated with rotting on the inside of its walls. From the outside it looked fine and dandy, but on the inside, it needed some serious help.

After my doctor and I went through almost 20 sheets of paper, poring over lab results and going over every single thing that was tested, I broke down. I cried bittersweet tears at the realization that I wasn't crazy. I wasn't attention-seeking or lazy or problematic. I was sick on the inside, and although my spirit was no longer in survival mode from my past, my physical body still was.

It is a sobering thought to realize that I had inadvertently been wanting for something that resembled an answer, any answer, to show up. And boy, did I get my wish.

However, some things were still inconclusive and further testing needed to be done. This is where the old me would fear. Yes, there is still angst at the unknown. But what I do know, now keeps me grounded.

I know that God loves me. I know that He is going to do a great work through me. I know that I have only just begun on the journey that

He has prepared for me. And I know that with God by my side, there is nothing to fear at all.

We are praying for healing, because through God anything is possible. Yet, I also know that God has imbued me with such strength that I can overcome anything that comes my way. That through The Spirit, I am energized and refreshed.

God's Plan Is Sovereign

This new journey of the unknown, will very well just be another part to my testimony. I will faithfully walk this road, I will not resent, I will not ask questions, I will not shout out, "Why me Lord?!" as I have done so many times in my past.

I will stay hopeful, grounded in the truth of my faith. I will stay steady, and will not waiver from the Lord who loves me so.

This life will be filled with many excuses to allow doubt to cloud your judgment. We live in a fallen world, and it is important to remember that although our souls are eternal through Jesus's sacrifice, our bodies are not.

We need to be just as faithful in our broken times, as we are in our blessed times. The Lord wants to unlock a specific purpose in you. He is your biggest cheerleader and He wants you to Become!

There are many different questions that I know, while here on Earth, I will never get an answer to. There are things that have been burning on the tip on my tongue for over a decade now.

Questions that I wish God could just zap His answers into my brain.

But I also now recognize, after much spiritual maturing, that I do not need the answers to these questions. That getting an answer to something, does not by any means change the outcome of a situation.

I have experienced abuse in my life. And for a long time I wanted to know why. I would yell at God and demand answers, "Why me?!"

I am an alcoholic. My body cannot handle alcohol like the average person, and I have a very adverse reaction. For so long I wanted to know why could I not drink a glass of wine like most women? Why could I not have alcohol in moderation without overdoing it to the point of blacking out? Why did I crave that stupid sugary drink like it was my own personal brand of heroine? I would get so upset at God, crying out to Him, "Why?!"

I have struggled with serious depression and anxiety throughout my life. There have been days when even the thought of getting out of bed and suffering through another day gave me a full-on breakdown. Where getting too close to a car when driving would make me have a panic attack and flashbacks of horrible car accidents. Where even sending a simple text message spiraled me into a debilitating toxic cycle of overthinking what I said and what the receiver on the other line must think of me.

These types of mental struggles crippled my ability to live out a regular lifestyle, and I would ask God "why" He allowed me to deal with these ongoing issues.

Since being a little girl I have had many bizarre health issues. I have broken more bones than I can count and I am always getting sick. I broke my first bone (my leg) before age 1. I had to spend a few weeks in the hospital for a rare disease called Cat Scratch Fever at age 4. I even had to have a colonoscopy at age 9. The health issues over the years have only persisted, each being something different and equally strange and bizarre. And now that I am dealing with another very difficult one, I am tempted to shout out again my frustrated WHY?!

But although I have all of these questions, that I would prefer to be answered, I know the general consensus of the responses I would receive.

> *"No test or temptation that comes your way is beyond the course of what others have had to face. All you need to remember is God will never let you down; he'll never let you be pushed past your limit; he'll always be there to help you come through it." (1 Corinthians 10:13 HCSB)*

I know the Lord created me to be strong. I know that He is not going to allow me to suffer through anything that will truly break me. I know that all of this pain is for a greater cause than my own personal comfort. These are some of the answers that I believe God would have supplemented me with anyways.

The Lord's plan is so vast and infinite. Like a thousand-piece puzzle, each tiny puzzle piece helps to contribute to a whole grand picture. If even one of those miniscule pieces were missing, then the puzzle would be incomplete. The image would look funny and fail to evoke the same kind of awe.

God created me to have a testimony that is complex and layered. That has many different aspects that will help me to contribute to relating towards others. My wonderful and supportive husband pointed this out to me the night that the doctor called us and let us know that the fine-needle biopsy did come back positive for malignant thyroid cancer.

Jake hugged me tight and whispered lovingly into my ear that I am going to have yet another battle title to add onto my already long repertoire. "Now you will be able to say that you are also a cancer survivor on top of everything else." He gazed down at my tear-stained rosy cheeks, with warm milk chocolate brown eyes, radiating love and support.

And as a sweet friend whom I just got off the phone with said, "At first I couldn't understand why it had to be you, because you've already gone through so much. But then I understood that you, out of anyone, would be the perfect person because you are so strong and keep your faith steady in God no matter what."

I am not special. Although my specific list of struggles might be a little unique, we all have things that we suffer through. There are so many others out there right now that are struggling with mental illness, addiction, cancer, abuse, and so much more.

I am not alone and neither are you!

Firstly, God is always with us even when we cannot feel His presence. And secondly, I am beginning to learn that there are so many people who suffer in silence.

In my past, I used to hide my sins and struggles, afraid that if I spoke them aloud I would be all the weaker for it. But after God humbled me and demanded that I be vulnerable, I was able to find so much strength in community. By opening up with my family members, I was able to learn that some of them also struggled with alcoholism and were living a lifestyle of sobriety.

By being willing to share my struggles openly, I was able to make friends and gather in fellowship with others who not only sympathized with me, but also understood the depth of my experiences. Just the knowledge that you are not alone in your brokenness is a cathartic type of healing that cannot be put into words. By getting more involved with my church community, I was able to stand strong with a group of believers who held one another up when one in the community began to stumble.

> *"Two people are better off than one, for they can help each other succeed. If one person falls, the other can reach out and help. But someone who falls alone is in real trouble. Likewise, two people lying close together can keep each other warm. But how can one be warm alone? A person standing alone can be attacked and defeated, but two can stand back-to-back and conquer. Three are even better, for a triple-braided cord is not easily broken." (Ecclesiastes 4:9-12 NLT)*

One of the first things I have done since being diagnosed with thyroid cancer was reach out to my God family and to our home churches, our OG church home back in Austin called Shoreline and our new wonderful church home up in Portland called Mannahouse.

Jake and I did not reach out to them for pity, as that is the last thing that I want. But we felt it important to reach out to them for prayer. Because of the pain that I am in, the doctors are worried that the cancer has spread to other parts of my body. We want to armor up with our God family and have as much prayer as possible that the cancer is contained solely to the thyroid gland.

There is a story in the Bible that I thought of when asking all of our church family to be our prayer warriors. It's a story in Mark, about a father who is desperate for Jesus to heal his son who is possessed by evil spirits. The man begs for help if Jesus is able to, as the disciples proved that they could not rebuke the spirit. I love our Savior's response to him.

"What do you mean, 'If I can'?" Jesus asked. "Anything is possible if a person believes." The father instantly cried out, "I do believe, but help me overcome my unbelief!" (Mark 9:23-24 NLT)

Jesus then strongly commands the spirit to leave the boy. Later when the disciples are confused about why they were unable to cast away the spirit themselves, our Lord explains to them.

"This kind can be cast out only by prayer." (Mark 9:29 NLT)

The power of prayer is more mighty than is even conceivable. And modern day miracles are possible, you best believe that!

God, Jesus, and the Holy Spirit are capable of anything and everything! But prayer is also immensely important. God wants us to come to Him with our problems and ask for His help. The more people who are speaking to the Lord about a similar issue, the better.

There is no shame in admitting that you are broken in a certain area. If anything, I think that shows you have tremendous courage, strength, and bravery. Just as it was not good in the book of Genesis for Adam to be alone. God does not want any of us to be alone either.

The devil comes to steal, kill, and destroy, but God is here to restore. He does not want any of His children to find themselves isolated or lonely in their struggle. He wants us to personally put on His armor every day and to also stand in a vast armada of other strong, armored-up and ready-to-fight believers.

Jesus did not walk on this Earth alone. No, He had His disciples encouraging Him, helping Him, and aiding in the good work that He was doing.

We need to stand strong in a group of believers so that when they find themselves fighting in the depths of a valley, we are there to help walk with them through it. And so that when the time comes that we are suffering a heartbreak or tragedy, we have others who love us, to help encourage us to keep going and to keep fighting faithfully for the Lord our God.

Time To Soar

I keep seeing butterflies everywhere. Since my cancer diagnosis, I have encountered more butterflies than I can even count. They each are so graceful, flitting around whimsically without a care in the world.

I have been noticing them in all different shapes and colors, but the ones that stick out to me the most are the beautiful yellow ones. The majestic Swallowtail. These large bright creatures bedazzle the clear blue sky with their enchanting pop of color. The yellow butterflies have the largest wings, commanding the power of a small bird.

I know that the recent reoccurrences of the influx of butterflies into my life is God's way of saying to me, "You can still fly sweet child."

I will admit that this recent news has made my heart feel a little heavy. It is one thing to know that your body is not healthy, but it is entirely another to be slapped with a label that has such a negative connotation associated with it.

The ugly C-word. Cancer.

Just the thought of it makes me shudder; like a foreign object that I know should not be there, I can pinpoint where the cancer has invaded my body. It feels like a heavy ache, weighing me down from the inside. My soul recognizes that it is toxic, that these cancer cells should not be there. That this tumor, the one that is making it hard to talk and keeping me up late into the night in pain, needs to be removed.

I know that surgery is necessary, and I know that I need to have it done within the next month. But I am still hesitant. Like an addict who knows that their vice is slowly killing them, yet they continue to have a hard time letting it go.

My motto has always been to be as natural as possible. To eat plant-based, gluten free, organic, vegetable-dense meals, while really limiting the amount of processed foods that I consume. Over the past couple of years, I have also been working to eradicate all of the chemicals from our home and believe it or not, chemicals are located everywhere! They are in our cleaning products, drinking water, bathing essentials, makeup, toothpaste, and so much more.

It has been a tiresome process, but I felt the Holy Spirit pushing me to make this transition a priority.

Now I can truly begin to understand why. I am able to appreciate that God was preparing me for this very moment. For a time when I unquestionably do need to eradicate all of the chemicals that I am exposed to. That I need to be very careful and cautious in regard to my immune system, diet, and chemical exposure.

I can indisputably acknowledge that the Lord was preparing me, so that this transition would not be as much of a shell shock to both myself and Jake.

I also now recognize why the Lord was so adamant in demanding that I move to Oregon. He wanted me to have steadfast faith in Him.

I know that God called me here so that I could be led to the doctor who was destined to discover my cancer. God knew all along that this disease would be a part of my story, and He is such a loving Father that He commanded I go to the place where I could find answers. Where eventually hope and healing could be provided to me.

Cancer is a scary thing, no matter the type or stage of cancer that a person has. Just the sobering realization that there is something toxic in your body. Something deadly and contagious, that has killed millions of people before you and will, unfortunately, kill masses of others after you.

It is painful both physically and spiritually to be reminded of just how fragile and mortal you truly are.

Today I was looking up at a big, beautiful, yellow butterfly and I watched as it began to fly higher and higher until I could no longer distinguish its presence. I was given somewhat of a raw realization. God has given each of us the ability to fly. He created us all with our own wings and wants us to allow Him to take us to new heights.

But one day, something will happen for each and every one of us, as God doesn't discriminate. One day the Lord will guide us to a height that we had never previously reached. He will have our glorious butterfly wings carry us above the puffy white clouds and into His everlasting light.

Like the butterfly that I admired today and then lost sight of, one day my wings will carry me so far up that I will no longer ever take a flight back down.

The journey to everlasting life.

Now, I don't know when that remarkable flight will take place. It could happen in a few weeks or in many decades from now. Recently, I've been reminded that my journey on Earth is simply the first chapter to my story. That the flights I go on with my wings here on Earth are just a practice for the eternity of soaring I will be doing in Heaven.

Life is too short to miss out on the purpose that God has for you. It is too fleeting to waste your precious time here on Earth. What you do now will greatly impact and determine what responsibilities and honors you will have in Heaven.

A small amount of suffering during your mortal life is nothing compared to an eternity of bliss and glory in Heaven.

If God has to continue to broaden my horizon of experiences so that I can encourage and relate to more audiences, then so be it. I will accept His will and faithfully trust in His plan. If I have to suffer so that

I can be truly heard by someone who is also suffering, then my pain will not even compare to the glory that Jesus is working through me.

I know that my strength does not come from this world. No, my strength comes from a Heavenly outlet, powered by never-emptying faith. I am not alone; I know my Father has a plan for me that is so intricate that He has deemed it necessary to only unveil it a little at a time.

"Your word is a lamp for my feet and light on my path."
(Psalms 119:105 HCSB)

We are not meant to know all of the major events that will take place in our lives before they happen. We are not intended to see the Fruit of what we will reap before we have planted a garden and sown good seed.

That is the beauty of God, that although we know nothing, our loving Father is all-knowing.

This verse was the first Bible verse that I ever memorized. And now I am starting to understand it with a different level of clarity. Jesus is with us, through all of our hardships. He is the light to the inevitable darkness we will experience here on Earth.

However, Jesus isn't the type of overhead fluorescent light that you flick on and is blinding, illuminating everything in a room. Because, although Jesus of course has that power, this is not the light that He offers His followers.

No, Jesus is a lamp to our feet, illuminating our steps so that we will not stumble in the darkness encamped around us. Jesus is a light on the path that the Lord has plowed out, specifically for you. The entire path is not lit up, although that would make it a lot less daunting to travel. But we are called to follow this path with blind faith, and Jesus will light the way a little at a time.

Had I known that almost as soon as I earned my beloved butterfly wings and started living out the life that I had only previously dreamed of, that I would get very sick and be diagnosed with cancer?

I know without a doubt, God called me to Portland so that I could be diagnosed and healed.

No, of course not.

This is the last thing I thought possible. But am I allowing this diagnosis to shake my faith, disrupt my beliefs, or change the way I am going to serve the Lord? Heck no!

I know God is playing out His plan for my life, and even though I don't quite understand it, I know that there is a purpose behind everything that we endure. I know that Jesus, my Prince of Peace, is here with me. That when I get overwhelmed, pained, or have a heavy and weary heart, Jesus wraps me up into His arms and hugs me tight, washing a tidal wave of soothing comfort over my distraught self.

I know that the Holy Spirit has got my back, that my gift for discernment is directly from Him and ultimately leading me straight toward healing, and that I only was able to discover this diagnosis by persevering and listening to the encouragement that was being spoken into my heart.

I know without a doubt that I was called to Portland, Oregon so that I could be diagnosed and ultimately healed. Amen to that!

God has got me. These are all just small details to a much bigger plan. Cancer is just another part of my testimony. Yes, I am still human. I have feelings, tears of uneasiness, and sometimes just feel uncertain about the "why's" surrounding these types of challenging situations. But God doesn't want me to bother with the "why's", He simply wants either a yes or no answer from His children.

"Will you accept that My son died on the cross for your sins?"

Yes.

"Will you follow Me faithfully, trusting in Me no matter where your path on Earth may lead?"

Yes.

"Will you waver in faith when you encounter suffering or hardship?"

No.

God makes it simple for us. The answers to His questions really are that easy. All I need to do is anchor myself to Him during this time. I need to dive headfirst into His word, release all of my worries and fears to Him in prayer, and never (not even for a second) allow the enemy to grab hold of my mind and allow me to feel sorry for myself.

Victimization is a strategic tactic from the enemy to keep you down. To stop you from neither discovering or using your beautiful wings. You were made to fly, not to be trapped on the ground.

Do not allow yourself to get stuck in your circumstances. Do not allow the suffering of your life to act as super glue, trapping you to a place that is lower than where you were created to live.

I choose to fly. Better yet, I am going to soar.

My wings may sometimes get tired, but that sure isn't going to stop me. God is my strength and as long as He allows me, I will keep flapping my wings and going wherever the wind of the Holy Spirit decides to carry me.

Find Bravery Through Your Trials

I learned something today that I find both ironic and interesting. On account of my upcoming thyroidectomy, a surgery to remove the cancer in my body which also means removing all of my thyroid, I have been doing a whole bunch of research.

As a journalism major, I research everything. I like to be very knowledgeable, informed, and well-versed on the subjects in my fields of expertise. AKA healthy living, natural medicine, environmental issues, a Christian lifestyle, and the life of Jesus.

With the things that are going on in my body, I have been spending hours learning all about what my body is currently going through and is about to have to go through with this surgery. I have met with multiple doctors and barraged them with educated questions, stunning both them and my husband who doesn't understand how overnight I can become an amateur expert in whatever I put my mind to.

Anyways, while researching all there possibly is to learn about thyroid cancer I came across something that stupefied me. Just like every other cancer, there is an awareness month for this type of cancer (September) and there is a ribbon with the designated thyroid cancer colors of purple, pink, and teal. But there is also a certain symbol that is associated with thyroid cancer. Almost like a mascot, so to speak.

And believe it or not, guess what it is?

Well, it's a butterfly of course. And I swear, I had no idea!

The butterfly, the comprehensive symbol of all of my metaphors and analogies. The reason I am writing this book. The butterfly that symbolizes becoming who God has created you to be.

How ironic. No, how God-ronic.

It's like God knew all along that I would be in the middle of my *Become* butterfly book when I got diagnosed with thyroid cancer. That this was just yet another puzzle piece, to that big picture that He is creating with the different moments of my life.

You see, the thyroid organ looks similar to a butterfly because of its two side lobes. It is located at the base of your neck and helps to regulate many body functions relating to your growth, development, and metabolism. Before all of this thyroid discernment, research, and now cancer diagnosis, I was like most people and didn't really understand what the thyroid actually did.

It's surreal that the butterfly has turned out to be this important to me because of the double meaning that I can take from it. That decades ago, when the butterfly first became an obsession, God knew all along and was preparing me for this moment where I would realize that the symbolic butterfly would become more meaningful to me than I ever thought possible.

While the butterfly inside of me (my thyroid) is going to be surgically removed and permanently taken out of my body, the butterfly that has metaphorically transformed on the outside is just learning how to fly. My time as a butterfly has finally come. And just like how after a real butterfly is done with its metamorphosis it must struggle to break free of its no-longer useful chrysalis, I must now struggle through cancer to strengthen my wings.

If the butterfly did not battle greatly to rid itself of its no-longer needed cocoon, then it would not strengthen and develop its new muscles that are necessary in order for the butterfly to take flight. The little winged creature would inevitably end up ground-ridden and dead if this endeavor did not ensue.

I need to get this sickness out of my body. I need to rid myself of my no-longer needed chrysalis. I won't be able to survive and fly if I stay in a toxic, unhealthy state. I need my physical butterfly to be removed from me so that my metaphorical and spiritual butterfly can soar.

I know this may sound silly. But these revelations are actually quite huge and impactful to me. The thought of this struggle that I am going through, being for a bigger purpose and contributing to God being able to morph me into who He has all along designed me to be, is what gives me strength.

It's what encourages me to keep going. To faithfully follow my Lord no matter the dark routes and windy paths His way may lead me through.

God needs me to embrace this sentiment. He knows that these are the things that enable me to type this message out to you. To be courageous and brave and vulnerable with you all. To share my story even if it's hard for me. To be honest about my past and shortcomings, even if some of the people who end up reading this don't like it. Because the fact of the matter is that there will always be someone who doesn't like me. Someone who is offended or doesn't believe in the message the Holy Spirit is prompting me to share.

But you know what? That's okay. Because there is also going to be someone who relates to what I have been through. Or someone who needed to hear the message that Jesus is speaking through me.

And that, that right there, is what makes this all worth it.

I am not here to make money. I am not here to become famous, or some television personality. I am just here to be me. To be your flawed, perfectly imperfect sister in Christ. I want to label myself as a woman after God's own heart. I just want to be able to show others the unexplainable love, redemption, and hope that is waiting for them on the other side of that cross.

I want you to know the love that has saved my life. I pray that these words will help you to grow deeper into relationship with God. To be able to grow more confident in who you were created to be, not who you think you "should" be.

I pray you, yes you, sweet friend, are truly opening your heart to be led and changed. That you work to embody the different aspects of the Fruit of the Spirit. God has utterly and absolutely changed my life, and I truly hope that you will allow Him to do the same for you.

You deserve it. No, you have not earned it, but it is yours for the taking. You get the opportunity to live forever in paradise.

What could be better?

You get the opportunity to stop feeling like you have to be in control of everything.

I mean come on, isn't that a nice thought?!

You get the chance to have all of your wildest dreams fulfilled, AND you get the opportunity to help spread the best news in the entire world. How could you not want to step into that type of glory?

Sometimes the most beautiful moments in life aren't when we are doing something brave or achieving anything great, they are when we silence the world around us and recognize our living God at work in our lives.

Become The Butterfly

This morning I woke up to the soft pitter-patter on the roof, a soothing melody that helped to gently stir me from my slumber. As I padded out of bed, the first thing I did when I got into the living room was open up all of the curtains.

You see, Jake and I are currently staying in a cozy little log cabin out on Mt. Hood, in Oregon. We are surrounded by tall, towering trees here in the dense forest. This adorable, quaint, wood-filled cabin reminds me of a combination of every single comforting camping movie I've ever seen. Lush green foliage surrounds me, with the canopy of branches glistening like diamonds from the raindrops lightly falling from the sky.

Jake has set off to find us some coffee, as somehow that is the one thing we forgot to bring (I know–gasp!), and here I am soaking up the peace in the stillness of this moment. Usually I would play some Frank Sinatra, do a Bible study on my phone, or find something else to keep me busy during this time of being alone. However, I feel God beckoning me to be still.

To be calm, in knowing that He is Lord God. Sometimes the most beautiful moments in life aren't when we are doing something brave or achieving anything great, they are when we silence the world around us and recognize our living God at work in our lives.

I know that I am protected and that He is here with me. I know that I am not alone, and that I matter - all of my problems and mishaps included. That I have not gotten lost in the shuffle of people that He watches over, that my Father knows my name specifically, and that He is rooting for me to become all that He has created me to be.

It has taken a very long time for me to come to this place of humble acceptance toward whatever my testimony may become. I am a vessel. I am not in control of my destiny, but I sure as heck am open to the ride. The Lord created me for a very specific reason, and I believe that I am just beginning to uncover the surface of that.

> *"To all who mourn in Israel, he will give a crown of beauty for ashes, a joyous blessing instead of mourning, festive praise instead of despair. In their righteousness, they will be like great oaks that the Lord has planted for his own glory." (Isaiah 61:3 NLT)*

I have found that God creates beauty out of chaos. That He is fully capable of turning my mess of a past into my message, and that by sharing that message, I will be obeying exactly what He is anointing me to do.

You see, as a butterfly, who has worked and waited for what seemed like a lifetime, the Lord has given me a multitude of different insights on the matter that I feel He is calling me to share.

I did not wake up one day with wings, as much as I had wished that were so. This entire process was a lot messier, and more complicated, than a fairytale sentiment such as that.

I lived as a dirt-crawling caterpillar for a very long time, foraging for survival. Trying to get to high places, but always ending back up on the ground.

One day I reached the point where I could "eat" no more. I was not being fulfilled by my old ways of living and thinking. I was starving for something more. I no longer fit in with those around me, who were living in ways much the same as myself.

I began to feel like a loner, not knowing why I did not like the very things that used to make me happy. My sense of perceived identity was being destroyed, and unbeknownst to me, being completely restructured.

Like an old dilapidated New York building that is demolished with a large wrecking ball, a new foundation was needing to be poured, and an entirely new infrastructure was needing to be built in the place where the old building once stood.

This time was very confusing for me at first. I felt very lost in the world, not sure of who I truly was or what I was meant to do. My life goals and dreams began to shift and everything that I had thought to be true about my way of living was turning out to be a false, unfulfilling sham.

I now recognize this is how we know that God is trying to work through us. When we no longer find joy in our worldly sin-filled ways, the Holy Spirit is at work trying to reset our hearts. My moral compass was being aligned, and the growing pains that came along with that were uncomfortable, to say the least. But stay strong sister, because when life gets turned upside down, you must not lose faith.

Remember, the caterpillar grows its wings during a season of isolation and change.

I went through a period of confusion and disorientation, while God was trying to snuff out the sin and rework me in His own image. This transformation process was coupled with feelings of disassociation of the "old" me, while feelings of uncertainty as the "new" me began to form within my cocoon.

During this time, I had to withdraw. I had to put a halt on all of the moving parts of my life and completely clear off the whiteboard. I had to take everything off my plate so that I could give God the opportunity to show me the things that needed to stay and the things that had best go.

You see, you must be willing to give up the caterpillar, in order to become the butterfly.

I became an empty slate before the Lord, open to whatever He wanted to mold out of me. I was his clay, and with me, I was giving Him the freedom to make what He wanted. It was a very transformative time in my life, filled with moments of discomfort, as the Lord was stretching my boundaries on who I thought I was meant to be.

My preconceived notions about my existence were thrown out the window and replaced with knowledge of the prize I was to my Father. There were many growing pains, but I stayed diligent during the process.

My wings began to form, thus allowing my life to take shape in a way I had only previously dreamed of.

Beloved, what if the very change that you have been avoiding is the one that gives you your wings?

I know that I am no longer a caterpillar. I feel the change that has taken place within my soul, the undeniable transformation of spirit.

The beautiful butterfly represents faith, rebirth, and the acceptance of new beginnings.

Although on the outside, I still look more or less the same. Curious, almond-shaped light brown eyes and unruly, long, dirty blonde hair. My soul could not be more different. No longer am I a citizen of this world, but I am a citizen of Heaven.

My wings have arrived.

The funny thing is, I know now my wings had always existed inside of me, as I was destined to fly. The dreams I have were planted in my heart for a very specific reason.

I just had to allow God to help uncover them.

And although it was such a struggle to get through my caterpillar stages, through many rough molts, it was even more difficult to cocoon myself up in the dark lonely chrysalis, with God transforming everything about me and not knowing what the end result would look like.

It was a very isolating time, but extremely necessary in the metamorphosis God was taking me through. The butterfly is proof that we sometimes have to go through a great deal of darkness in order to become something extraordinary.

Alas, that transition period was long and heavy, but I finally emerged victorious with my wings.

I have begun to emerge from my now unneeded tomb, still struggling at times to break free from a former version of myself that I no longer identify with.

A butterfly is still very delicate initially. After it develops wings, it continues to have a lot of growing to do. It is a battle to get free of the cocoon. But this struggle is extremely necessary in order for the butterfly to develop the muscles it needs to be able to fly.

I am currently exercising spiritual muscles that I didn't even know I possessed, slowly but surely allowing the Spirit to teach me how to fly.

I know I still have a very long way to go. I know that my wings are currently minuscule inexperienced butterfly wings, fresh and new. But I also know that I was meant to soar. That I will fly high into the sky, gazing excitedly at the beautiful world around me.

I know I will fly over the places that I used to reside in my undeveloped caterpillar state, but instead of regretting what I had to go through to earn my wings. I now look at it all as a journey.

If my struggle were to have been taken away from me, my victory would also have been robbed. I would not be who God created me to be without the battles that I fought through. I would not have half as much of a message to spread or testimony to share, if my suffering did not exist.

I believe God created me to be stronger than I can even comprehend. He knew that my life would not always be easy, but He was giving me these experiences to share with those who also have lived and survived through hardships.

My story is no better or worse than yours. My sins no dirtier. We are all alike in God's eyes. And no matter what stage of life you find yourself in, whether you are a caterpillar craning your head hoping for your wings or you are a seasoned flier, who has been soaring for a long time but forgot where it was you were supposed to be going. It's never too late to let God guide you again, to allow Him to work something wonderful in you that you neither expected or believed possible.

The time is **now** to dedicate yourself towards the greatness you were created to do for your Kingdom.

Sometimes when I see butterflies in training, caterpillars that are still growing, I remember that I too was there, not very long ago. A butterfly should never look back at a caterpillar in shame.

Our journey is who we are. Our past is a vital key towards the transformation we were each destined for.

I try to encourage those around me to not give up faith, to never stop trying harder to grow closer to your God who loves and cherishes you.

God wants you to level up.

The secret ingredient is that you really have to *want* to change. We only have a certain amount of time here on Earth, and how fulfilling would it be to finally begin on the mission that we were sent here to do? I believe that we all will be pleasantly surprised at how much we can achieve with Jesus guiding our steps.

> *"Trust in the Lord with all your heart, and do not rely on your own understanding; think about Him in all your ways, and He will guide you on all the right paths." (Proverbs 3:5-6 HCSB)*

Your time as a caterpillar has expired. It's time to let that season of your life come to a close. Your wings are waiting for you. God is ready for you to fly. He will take you higher than you could ever imagine, to places that are even better than your wildest dreams.

This, right here right now, could be your butterfly moment.

The awakening that you needed to be brave enough to let go of your no-longer hospitable caterpillar self. To be willing to change and transform, so that your Heavenly Father can reward you with your wings.

Good is simply not good enough. You were destined for greatness. Don't miss out on the beautiful creature you were intended to become.

Ask yourself this, are you open to receiving your Master's blessing?

Fly High Baby

I don't know where you are in your life, so I'm not going to pretend that I do.

But what I do know, I feel inclined to share and encourage you with. You are on this Earth for a very important reason.

Not to get hundred of likes on your posts. Not to make a boatload of money. And most definitely not to have a perfectly toned, runway model body.

You are here to make the world a better place. To spread light and love. To tell others of your Heavenly Father and the everlasting life He offers.

God wants to be represented by you. He wants you to sponsor His message through your life's work. God wants our steps to be with the Spirit, as He is calling us to live by His word each and every day that we are here on Earth.

> *"Since we live by the Spirit, we must also follow the Spirit."*
> *(Galatians 5:25 HCSB)*

Through our fruit-filled lives, our intention should be to glorify the Father.

> *"My Father is glorified by this: that you produce much fruit and prove to be My disciples." (John 15:8 HCSB)*

By taking a realistic examination of your heart's condition, you will be able to discover ways in which you can grow closer to God. A very apparent way to uncover if your faith is growing or stagnant is to judge how evident the Fruit of the Spirit is in your life.

You were created to be kind to others. To love all those around you, including children, animals, and yes, even the environment. The Earth is your garden to nurture.

It's your duty to help other individuals to blossom, flourish, and grow.

If you live your entire life with a "me" mindset, then you will find yourself very lonely and dissatisfied with the end results. But if you live with an "others" mindset, you will not only see your own dreams begin to be fulfilled, but you will have the joy of helping others to realize and chase after their dreams too.

If I can just help to motivate and inspire *one* person to love God, and enable them to allow the healing that He provides, then I will be satisfied.

Of course, my goal is to take part in leading so many more people to the grace and love of Jesus. But all it takes is one.

One moment to accept Christ as your Lord and Savior. One decision to change the entire trajectory of your life - to no longer be a citizen of the world, a falling crumbling place, but to be a citizen of Heaven, welcomed into the Pearly Gates of eternity.

Are you ready to make the best decision of your existence?

I want to see you one day in Heaven. I want to worship the Lord with you. I want to continue to grow with you.

I truly love you, my sweet sister in Christ. Please join me, towards becoming who you have always been meant to be.

The time has come, and what an exciting realization that is.

It's time to spread your wings and **soar.**

A Prayer For New Life

Although I grew up going to church, I still felt very distant from God in my late teens and early twenties. In my mind, if God truly cared for me, I would not have been used and abused like I had. I would not have struggled with debilitating depression and anxiety. I would not be struggling through addiction, feeling trapped in my immense sin. These heartbreaking situations made me question whether God truly loved me, whether I was even worthy of that love to begin with. I found myself lost in the world, jaded and shutting out the Goodness of our Father. I thought I was alone, but I now recognize that toxic mentality was a lie from the enemy. God had always been pursuing my heart, I had just been continuously refusing the Heavenly aid that was being graciously offered to me.

Through a domino effect of misfortunate events, my pride was broken and I was humbled to my knees. I had hit rock bottom and the darkness surrounding me was too much to handle. I knew I needed God.

The problem was that I was confused on how to fully submit to God. I didn't want to go to a church and walk up to the front during an altar call. I didn't feel like raising my hand and repeating after the pastor in a formal setting. I was timid and scared, afraid of how to go about the biggest decision of my life.

Through my tears, and on my knees in my cat-hair filled condo,

I cried out to our God. I told Him of my pain, I shared with Him the burden of my grief. I asked for help and I submitted myself to accepting that Jesus DID die on the cross for my sins. And although I will never be worthy of that sacrifice, He did it because He loves me. He will always love me no matter what I do, or how many times I forsake Him.

Suddenly my soul felt an intense lightness, I felt Jesus reaching down to grab my hand and lift me out of that dark pit.

Accepting the Lord into my heart was the best decision I could ever make. Allowing the sacrifice that Jesus made for my sins to cleanse me, saved my life. More than anything, I desire for you to experience His overflowing goodness too.

I'd like to invite you to pray this salvation prayer with me today:

Lord Jesus, I thank you for sacrificing your life on the cross to atone for my sins. Thank you for rescuing me from sin and death, by offering your gracious forgiveness. Please create in me a new heart. I no longer want to be a citizen of this fallen world, I choose to be a citizen of Heaven.

I surrender my life to you Jesus, the highest name. I give my heart, my soul, my spirit, my mind, my body, and everything in my name to the Kingdom of God.

I promise to follow you Christ to be my King, to be my Savior, and to by my friend, as long as I shall live. Today and forever, I repent from my ways, the world's ways, and the enemies ways, all for the praise and glory of God the Father, Jesus the Son, and the Holy Spirit.

In Jesus' name, Amen.

I love you, sweet friend. All of Heaven is rejoicing alongside us over your choice to accept God's love into your heart. This decision will forever change your life for the better. Thank you for joining me on this journey. I know the Lord is going to do many great works through you.

About the Author

Madison Panko is on a mission to help others who have also fallen upon hard times but have found redemption through the love of God.

She is an author, blogger (www.thehappyhotmess.com), freelance writer, and business professional. Throughout every position that Madison has ever worked, she has allowed her God-given gift of writing to shine through and enabled her creativity to assist her to excel in whatever job position she holds.

She leads small groups within her community by eloquently intertwining her story with the lessons of the Bible. Madison works hard to be vulnerable and open with everyone she meets. Accrediting all glory to her loving Father in Heaven.

Madison loves to volunteer in children's ministry and make an impact towards sharing compassion with children in need. She has served as a Board Member for the Human Trafficking and Exploitation Action Network. Madison has a passion for rescuing children from abuse and brokenness, and being part in helping to show them the light and restoration found in Jesus. Just like the Lord rescued her, and allowed her to blossom and grow, she now desires to use her public speaking and writing to help share His messages of hope, joy, and everlasting life.

She has a Bachelor's degree in Agricultural Communications and Journalism from Texas A&M University. She also worked for a local newspaper during her time in college, helping to share the stories of business owners living in the area. Her talent for connecting with her audience, and being a trustworthy confidant has enabled her to truly hone her writing craft and pursue excellence in this field.

When Madison is not pouring her soul into her writing or perched on the couch with a steaming cup of coffee, a Frank Sinatra record playing, and an enthralling book, she can be found hiking a lush Oregon trail with her adventure partner and loving husband Jake. Madison is an avid traveler, plant-based foodie, and animal lover. You can consistently find her curled up with her sassy rescue Maine Coon Stella, diving into the living word of God.

Aspiring to never stop growing with the Lord and finding ways to use her testimony to help others during times of brokenness and healing, everything Madison stands for and does is driven by her innate desire to bring hope and love to everyone around her.

 www.thehappyhotmess.com

Click on "Contact" to inquire about having Madison speak at your event.

 www.Facebook.com/AuthorMadisonPanko

 @MadisonPanko

If you enjoyed *Become,* I encourage you to equip yourself with **additional resource**s at

www.thehappyhotmess.com.

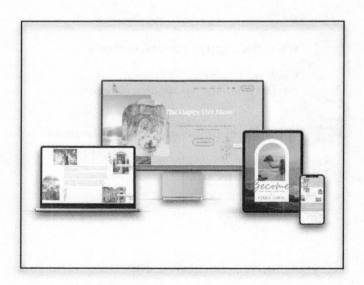

Don't miss additional material from Madison with the *Become* companion Study Guide & Discussion Questions!

Madison is passionate about coming alongside readers on their own journeys of discovering their true purpose. True and lasting growth comes from submitting yourself to the Lord and allowing Him to show you the carefully crafted plans He has destined for your life.

If you enjoyed this book, I encourage you to go deeper with the companion study guide and discussion questions that will enable you to truly discern where God wants to take you.

These free resources include group discussion questions, personal study, and journal reflection materials.

Made in the USA
Coppell, TX
24 March 2023